How to Talk to Women

*Get Her to Like You & Want You With
Effortless, Fun Conversation &
Never Run Out of Anything to Say!
How to Approach Women
(Dating Advice for Men)*

Ray Asher

Table of Content

Your Free Resource Is Awaiting

To better help you, I've created a simple mind map you can use _right away_ to easily understand, quickly recall and readily use what you'll be learning in this book.

Click Here To Get Your Free Resource

Alternatively, here's the link:

https://viebooks.club/freeresourcemind-mapforhowtotalktowomen

Your Free Resource Is Waiting..

Get Your Free Resource Now!

Introduction

Have you ever wanted to be able to effortlessly talk to a woman? To be able to have the ability to walk right up to her and have her become captivated by you and want to connect as you talk?

Why can't you? Is it nervousness or insecurity? Or do you think she's going to turn you down? Are you afraid that you won't know what to talk about?

I used to have that problem, but over the years, I discovered how to have stimulating and fulfilling conversations with women. Through trial and error and learning from my mistakes, I finally developed the ability to relate to women, talk and ensure that it was a stimulating conversation all while building my connection and chemistry.

Besides, I want to share what I have learned with you!

When I was young, I had no idea how to talk to women. I would bring up all the wrong subjects, I wouldn't listen carefully enough, and eventually, it became very clear that they were not interested in what I had to say.

Over time, I began to learn the secrets of communication with the opposite sex. It's not any magical trick or some overhaul of your life. It's simply applying some learned skills as well as making some changes to your mindset and approach.

It wasn't easy. There were many failures. But each time, I picked myself back up and learned from my experiences. I used all my resources, including books, the internet, and even female friends and began to change my approach and subject matter. I learned when to talk to a woman and how to strike up conversations using real, genuine topics and not stupid pick-up lines guaranteed to fail.

Most of all, I learned that at the basis of it all was my attitude and mindset. Therein was the key to what women responded to, that fire inside a man that made them want to get closer.

Now, I can have stimulating conversations with any woman at any time. I've learned what women respond to in a man and how to make sure it comes across to them. I've learned how to create situations and security in a woman so the conversation cannot only be more fun and flirtier but can also lead to more interaction, including getting her phone number, dates, and sex.

It's not just on the first meeting. It's also about having great conversations and being able to communicate on dates and even in relationships.

It's not impossible. You can do it. I'm going to reveal to you how to present yourself properly, create chemistry, and have the mindset that women want plus I'll help you learn how to talk with women online, how to learn things about her without her telling you, and how to steer the conversation where you want it to go.

When you are done reading this book, I know that you will have the confidence and tools to talk to any woman you meet.

So, read on and learn ***How to Talk to Women!***

Part One: The Fundamentals

Chapter 1: Your Mindset and How It Affects How People View You

Have you ever met someone who seemed nice and attractive but within five minutes of talking to him or her, they were so negative and crude that they actually looked ugly to you?

I remember once I met a model that I had actually seen in several men's magazines. She was blonde, tall, and every curve was in the exact right place. This woman was the idea of what I thought a woman should be physically. In short, she was gorgeous.

Then she opened her mouth.

Every word that spewed out was full of sarcasm and hatred. She had opinions on everything and, usually, it was how much she despised it. She even let out a few choice comments about people that could be viewed as nothing less than prejudice.

Within moments, I no longer saw the beautiful model but instead a truly foul, undesirable human being.

That's what happens when someone sees a negative mindset in a person. So, you need to make sure you are in a place where you put off positive vibes that women will respond to. **This is your mindset.**

Now, it doesn't mean you have to suddenly become Mr. Cheerful Optimist and think the world is a beautiful, flower-filled place. No, it just means that you are being positive, confident, and moving forward as a man.

Dangerous Mindsets

There are a number of pitfall mindsets that people can fall into that will destroy not just their social and interpersonal lives but can take them down in regards to their career and even their family.

Even more so, women pick up on these mindsets and are not going to be attracted to you or even interested in seeing you if you did have an initial connection.

The Victim

This mindset is when people believe that they are the target of the actions of other people. They tend to feel powerless and can fall into helplessness.

Women see this as weak and having a lack of control over your life. No woman is going to respond to you if they feel like you are spiraling downwards or blame others for what you should be handling.

Giving up your power and believing others caused your troubles is weak and very unsexy.

The Perfectionist

While everyone strains for being the best they can, a person with a perfect mindset isn't satisfied unless they are the best and can set exceptionally high standards for themselves. They begin to become scared that they won't accomplish their goals and therefore be judged a failure. Many times, it is one extreme or the other with no in-between.

Women can find a man with this mindset stressful. They may think that they have to live up to your standards or be uncomfortable with your outlook. Women want to be with someone who accepts them and doesn't judge them.

The "Hit the Wall"

This is the person who is burned out. Either due to work, life, or relationships, they have an attitude of giving up because their energy and emotional strength have been used up. This is seen in their work and relationships, as they don't have the will or energy to put in the work needed.

This mindset can easily lead to negativity and a sense of helplessness, and no one wants to be around that.

The Self-Entitled

This is a mindset where a person believes that they deserve whatever they desire simply because they feel they are owed. They can be incredibly selfish and narcissistic because of this attitude and will sometimes even go as far as hurting others (mentally if not physically) in order to get what they feel they deserve.

Your Reaction

Part of your mindset is how you mentally react to a situation. When you see a woman you want to talk to, what is the first thought that comes to mind?

Is it negative? Do you think that she doesn't want to talk with you, or do you assume that she is interested?

You can't have that reaction. Your first thoughts should be positive and genuine. Generally speaking, if your mindset is one that women find attractive, you are way ahead of the game. Mindset can often be more important than physical attraction.

Have you ever met a successful, positive guy who isn't the most attractive in the world but still does incredibly well with women? He doesn't have to be rich or drive an expensive car for women to like him.

It's his mindset that women are responding to. The way he thinks, reacts, and views the world. This can spark the desires in her brain and be far more powerful than his hair, face, or muscles.

Core Values

In order to truly be in a healthy and proper mindset, you need to discover what your core values are. These are the things that mean the most to you and the people around you.

They could be courage, pride, creativity, strength, empathy, or dozens of others, but you need to know that about yourself in order to be fulfilled and genuine. You'll have more confidence because you'll know who you are and what you stand for.

Mindsets Women Find Attractive

There are several different mindsets that women find most attractive. While they have differences, they all share the same quality of confidence and positivity.

Women respond to men on the move. Whether it's your job, desires, or just your general attitude, women like men who know what they want and how to get it. That is something all these mindsets share.

I have found that being the positive man has worked out best for me in the past. I have tried the fun guy, but sometimes it is hard to balance the line between fun guy and being too much. In a world of negativity, women are very attracted to a man who can be positive, one who doesn't spend his time complaining about life and the other people in it.

The Driven

Women want to find a man who has direction and knows what he wants to achieve. You might not be where you want to be yet, but you're on your way.

Don't try to fake it. Be genuine. Don't lie about the car you drive or that you run a company at 21. However, be open about your goals, dreams, and how you intend to accomplish them.

The Positive Man

This is the supportive man who is never a hater. He is a positive force for the people around him and they love to be around him. He genuinely cares for people and what happens to them.

The positive man is vocal about his support for people and cheering them on in their successes and helping during their failures. People (including women) love to be around guys with this mindset.

The Fun Guy

Life might not be a party, but this mindset always looks for the fun in a situation. He goes out of his way to have a good time and makes sure people around him do as well.

The Humble Man

This is the effortless man. Nothing fazes him and his own accomplishments are not something to brag about. He realizes that it's about the journey, not the destination, and isn't going to judge others.

The humble man doesn't need to blow his own horn, he lets his accomplishments speak for themselves. Women love the quiet glow of success these men put off.

The Leader

Leaders always rise to the top of a group. In fact, sometimes it's almost subliminal and others turn to them for advice without even knowing why.

It's not about being an alpha male (which we will delve into later), it's about being intelligent, strong, and behaving in a way that makes those around you secure in your abilities.

The Passionate Man

I've mentioned passion a few times in this book and my others. It's because, like confidence, it is one of the things that women respond to the most. If you are a passionate man, whether in work or life or both, women will react positively. It's one of the hallmarks of a successful man.

The Adventurer

You look for the road less traveled and the thrill of discovery. Women love this mindset because you aren't satisfied and are always looking for that new experience.

Chapter 2: Self Accountability and Self-Worth

Before you can really connect with another person, you have to be in touch with yourself. You have to have control over your emotions and really value who you are as a person.

If you don't, you are not only going to not attract the right woman, but you won't be able to keep her. In some cases, missing out on your own confidence is going to lead you to the wrong kind of woman. While you are out there looking for the right woman, you could inadvertently attract a toxic woman, the kind of woman who will prey on men who aren't all that confident or who will help them create the drama which they thrive on. This definitely isn't what you are looking for here.

You don't have to have it all together, but she needs to know that you have the tools and a plan to move your life forward before she's going to be interested in being a part of it.

How You Destroy Your Own Self-Worth

Sometimes as humans, we have a horrible habit of self-destruction. It might be because we don't believe we should succeed or possibly we are dealing with mental programming of low self-esteem going back to childhood.

There are many ways that we do this to ourselves and in order to be successful with the opposite sex, you need to purge these actions from your life.

You Use Alcohol as a Social Crutch

Look, I'm not passing judgment. I enjoy a drink as much as the next guy. But if you don't feel like you can be social without having a few, then something is not right. This includes marijuana, too.

We all grew up with the idea of "liquid courage," that if we have a couple of drinks, it will help with nerves and give us the power to be more sociable.

In college, a lot of people just take it as the way socialization works.

That's not help, that's dependency.

You need to take a serious look at what causes your anxieties and stop using alcohol to numb them. If it's deep-seated enough, you might even want to consider counseling. There is nothing wrong with seeking help for drinking dependency. It doesn't mean you are an alcoholic, it simply means that you have created some bad habits and you need to fix them before it's too late.

Keeping It Inside

As men, we are often taught that we should just stuff feelings down inside and push on. The problem is that this can be damaging to your mental health.

Now, I'm not saying you need to cry when you see weepy commercials, but you shouldn't keep stuff bottled up inside. Suffering a loss or some sort of emotional turmoil can be hard and keeping it inside gives your brain a horrible place to play it over and it will consume you.

It's ok to talk things out. Talk to your best friends. If they don't want to hear it, it might be time for new friends or even visiting a therapist. Again, it's manlier to control your problems than let them control you.

Dwelling on Inner Negative Messages

We all have internal messages in our brains that we play over and over. For a lot of guys, they are positive, motivational, or thoughts that push them forward. If you played sports, it's probably pretty likely your coach talked to you about visualization and positive outlook and how it can influence your ability on the field or the court.

Some men are continually listening to an internal message that tells them they are not good enough, or that they are always going to fail. Generally, this nagging inner voice is tearing them down and the toxicity multiplies.

Having your self-worth and confidence down means you are not going to do well in life and career, let alone with women. You need to get rid of the negative thoughts. Concentrate on your wins, goals, and successes. Plan how to get better at interacting with women (picking up this book was a great start!).

Just like sports, if you visualize positive results, you will begin to reshape your internal messages and your outlook will change.

Body Image

It isn't just women who have body image issues, men do as well.

It might be your weight or a receding hairline. There's nothing wrong with not being completely happy with your body. It's how you deal with it that can be the problem.

Don't fall for stereotypes that you have to look a certain way in order to be happy. If you want to lose some weight, do it. Take control and change your body. If there are other issues that you truly can't live with, then you have the right and ability to change them.

However, remember that no matter what you change physically, you are still you.

Avoiding Mental Health Problems

Many men won't admit that they may be having some problems. Depression is a very real issue and often guys won't get help, thinking that's not the manly way.

I disagree. I always believe the manly way is to take control of a situation and solve it. If you are suffering from depression or other mental problems, get some assistance. It's a very real condition that can lead to tragic results.

The news is full of stories of men who were seen as strong and masculine that secretly suffered from mental illness and ended their lives tragically. Don't be one of them.

Thinking You Are Helpless

Men like to have control. It's in our nature. But when things start to fall out of our control, sometimes we begin a spiral into helplessness.

If gone unchecked, then this can create an attitude of inaction and can even spiral into depression. Realize that there are some things you can't control, but your reaction and how you recover are completely up to you.

Shutting Out Other People

Isolation is terrible because it can avalanche. If things aren't going well or you are beginning to fall into depression or low self-esteem, you will most likely not want to be around a lot of people. That amplifies because the less you are around people, the less people you will meet and honestly, you may start to think you enjoy being alone. Being alone seems simpler without disappointment or troubles.

But that's not what is happening. You are developing a mental muscle memory of loneliness, and your brain is compensating and getting used to it. You are developing a bad habit, and you need to break it.

Pointing the Finger at Others

When you are having issues with your self-worth and esteem, it's easy to point a finger at other people and not take responsibility for your own actions or situation.

Even if someone else did something to you legitimately, you can only get so far with your own inner mental health by blaming them. Even the most tragic victim needs to eventually take back control of their life and make decisive choices to get on track.

How to Build Your Self-Esteem

The great thing about self-esteem and your own value is that you can rebuild it. People often think that once it's broken, your personality has changed and there is no way back to the top.

That is completely not true.

Believe in Yourself

This isn't a rah-rah pep speech. This is just a basic truth. You need to believe in your ability to make sound decisions and choices in life. Once you do this, you have made a major step forward.

Start with small victories and build on them. Sometimes, that's all it takes. Whether it's work, hobbies, or interacting with women, you need to truly believe that you can be successful in everything that you do.

Block Out the Negativity- External and Internal

It is easier said than done, but this is something you'll get better at with time. You need to shake off any external negativity from family, friends, the news, and even online. Any source that does not bring you up and support you. It's not going to be easy at first but maintain a positive outlook.

Also, work to quell any negative voices in your mind. Past experiences might tinge your self-esteem and make you think you can't do better or change things, but you always can.

Take Stock of Your Assets

Go positive. Think about all the things you have going for you. Your skills, abilities, and experiences. Focus on these and how they can help you and move you toward success.

If you are really down or trying to change, make an actual list. Be honest but also be positively truthful. Don't put yourself down or try to be humble with your list. You need to remind yourself of all the things that you have going for yourself. This list is for you. It's not bragging, it's taking stock.

Embrace Change

Change can be scary, but it's a great thing. Change allows you to grow and test yourself. If you go to the gym and always do the same exercise and the same amount of weight, you aren't challenging yourself and you won't move forward. It's the same with life.

Embrace change and the opportunities it gives you in work, personal life, and your inner self. Seek out opportunities to push yourself and take on new opportunities.

Believe You Should Be Happy

Sometimes when people get down or begin to lose their self-worth, they believe that's the way it should be. They start to think they don't have the right to be happy or they don't deserve it.

That's garbage!

Everybody deserves the right to be happy. Heck, it's in the Declaration of Independence. There is no measuring scale that says who does and doesn't deserve happiness.

Not believing you should be happy can also be very dangerous because you may turn to the wrong things to fill the hole you feel you have. If you aren't happy, you might look for fulfillment in drugs, alcohol, or dangerous and addictive sex.

Learn from Your Mistakes

We all screw up! When you make a mistake, learn from it. Acknowledge and make amends if need be but analyze what you did. What went wrong? What could you have anticipated that you didn't? What could you do differently so you don't repeat it?

How to Be Self-Reliant

At first glance, you probably think this section is about how to pay your bills, take care of yourself, and the like. That's part of self-reliance, but this is about accountability.

Self-reliance is also more than just having a job and paying your bills. It's about mentally being self-reliant and being able to solve problems in your life on your own without being rescued by others.

Make Your Own Decisions

When you are truly self-reliant, you make your own decisions about your future. Now, that doesn't mean that you need to plan everything and not allow others to arrange things or set them up.

It merely means that you are the one deciding about what you do and how you do it. It's about the direction your life takes and how to make sure it's what you want.

Don't Compare Yourself to Others

If you are judging yourself by the actions or successes of others, you are giving away your own worth. You can't achieve your personal goals and be independent when you let the actions or successes of others be the measuring stick for your own life.

You should be able to list things that you like about yourself that are totally separate from what others do. Try it and make sure that they aren't dependent on what you feel others have achieved.

Use Healthy Ways to Express Your Emotion

If you feel the need to take out your anger on people, you are not being self-reliant or acting in a healthy way. First of all, you need to be able to burn off steam or deal with anger and other emotions in a healthy way. This does not mean outbursts, violence, or going straight to arguments. Whether it's burning off some anger with physical exercise or learning to have constructive conversations with someone you are upset with, you have to have productive ways of emotional management.

Plus, think about it, if you have to have an outburst with a person in order to feel like you are dealing with an issue, you aren't being self-reliant, are you? You have to have that other person, which means you are giving away your power and independence.

Accept Responsibility

When you accept responsibility for your life and actions, it's a huge step toward self-reliance. It's only when you do this that you can take active steps toward personal growth.

Part of responsibility is also cleaning up the messes. As much as we want it to, life doesn't always go according to plan and in order to keep going, we have to deal with problems and issues. Part of being a self-reliant man is being able to handle them without your entire life crashing down.

Chapter 3: The Alpha Male- Truths and Myths

That's what women say they want. The Alpha Male. The confident, assertive man who always gets his way. They claim that it's genetic and primal that they want to be a pack leader.

Of course, there are those women who find the Alpha Male a big turnoff. They would rather have the considerate man, the thoughtful man, the sensitive man. But still, there seems to be a decent number of women who are interested in the alpha male personality type.

But what if I told you there is no such thing as the Alpha Male? At least, not the way people think?

The Alpha Male Myth

The term "Alpha Wolf" isn't real. It's based on the research of a scientist named L. David Mech, who wrote the book *The Wolf* in the 1970s based on his wolf observations at a wildlife preserve. Mech came up with the concept that there was one "alpha" wolf that was the dominant leader of all the other wolves. The book was a huge hit and coined the phrase "alpha wolf," which people began to apply to people. Their reasoning was that people must behave like wolves, even though we have no other connections to them.

After the book was released, Mech went back and studied wolves again but this time in the wild. He realized that he had been incorrect in his findings. Wolves don't have a dominant hierarchy the way he had assumed, he realized. He tried to make his findings public, but by then, it was too late. The idea of the "Alpha Male" had taken hold.

But that doesn't mean anything, right? The more aggressive, athletic, assertive guy is an alpha and he's going to always get what he wants in every situation, right?

Not always.

Imagine you are the star college quarterback. You are the most popular guy on campus. You're smart and you get good grades. Everything is great for you. You are the top dog.

Now, drop yourself in with the characters of the television show, *The Big Bang Theory*. Suddenly, you are at the bottom of the heap. You are in their world. You are definitely not the smartest and definitely not in charge. In fact, you might not even be able to keep up with the conversation.

If you are the alpha on the football field, you are definitely not trying to debate with that group. They are the alpha and you are now answering to them.

Being the "alpha" is situational, and it's really just a name for aggressive guys. It's not the be-all and end-all way of being. It's not something to aspire to.

Be yourself. Be confident in who you are, and you'll fall where you will.

Now, that being said...

The Lone Wolf

This is what I think a lot of women mistake for the Alpha Male.

They like the individual man who is responsible for his own life and circumstances. Being responsible when it comes to money, life, and your actions trigger something deep inside a woman. Remember that flirting and all of this is based on primal desires.

Deep down, she wants someone who knows how to get stuff done. With a bit of mystery, the interest deepens. The Lone Wolf doesn't care about being a leader or having others bend to his will. He is merely concerned with his own fulfillment and needs. His self-worth is high, but he realizes it doesn't matter what people think of him.

It's Not All About the Women

A Lone Wolf has a goal and he's not going to let a relationship stand in the way. It could be work, it could be a goal to sail around the world. To a woman, that determination is sexy.

While he's on his adventures, he's happy to have a woman at his side, but he's just as happy on his own. A woman doesn't define him.

You Know All Women Like You and You Don't Care

Women love lone wolves.

Young women, old women. Women in general. But the Lone Wolf plays it off. He accepts the attention, but he doesn't need it.

Showing Masculinity and Dominance

There was a time years ago when, if you asked what it meant to be a masculine man, people would have said things like chest hair, big muscles, and the ability to get any woman he wanted.

The concept of the Alpha Male became the stereotypical portrait of the perfect masculine male, but as I discussed earlier, that was a misunderstood ideal and was actually just one type of different masculine men.

But times change and the definition of what is masculine can shift. The same thing happens to women. There was a time if a woman didn't have the body of a teenage boy, they weren't considered feminine at all. Go back further in time, if they weren't what we considered overweight, they weren't seen as beautiful.

So, which traits are considered masculine and will show her you are a mature, respectable male?

Decisiveness

It's not just about knowing what you want, it's also about being able to think on your feet. It could be something as simple as choosing where or what to eat to how your schedule goes.

She doesn't want wishy-washy. She doesn't want to watch you stumble over decisions. However, this doesn't mean decide for her. Don't go to a restaurant and order her dinner for her. Yeah, I know, can you believe guys still try that?

But if you ask her where she would like to go to dinner and she says, "Oh, I don't know..." or "Wherever," don't get into a discussion. Take that as a hint to take the reins.

Better yet, when you ask her to dinner, tell her you'll take care of all the arrangements. Ask her if there is any food she dislikes and then take it from there.

Self-Reliance

Being masculine means you can take care of yourself. Whether it's work or clothing or just food, being a man means you can get stuff done for yourself.

Being "hangry" is a perfect example. Ever forget to eat to the certain point that you started acting like a jerk? Well, why? Because you didn't have the self-reliance to make sure you ate. Now, if you snap at her and just say that it's because you didn't eat, she may be nice on the outside about it but inside she's wondering how you can't even eat right.

Do you expect someone to be your mother and make sure you eat? Trust me, she does not want to be your mommy.

It's Real and Not an Act

Being masculine comes from within. It's not the clothes you wear or the way you style your hair.

I can't count how many guys I've run across in my life who weren't very masculine and decided to fix it externally by buying a leather jacket or a motor-cycle. That doesn't make you a man. Now you are just lacking masculinity with a new wardrobe and vehicle.

It shouldn't be shakable. You shouldn't suddenly show true colors so that people realize it was all an act. You need to start internally building confidence, habits, and outlook and it will become an organic part of who you are.

Masculinity Is Not Conformity

A masculine man knows what he wants and believes in. Different than the Alpha Male "he gets what he wants," this is about standing up for what you believe in.

You don't change your core beliefs or thoughts just because the rest of the people around you did. You stand up for your beliefs and will debate them. You don't mimic what other people say or believe. You are confident in your values and the way you view the world.

Real Men Learn

One of the hallmarks of maturity is not only learning from your mistakes but realizing there is information in the world that you don't know. It also means you accept it.

Part of being masculine, as we already discussed, is adapting and being self-reliant. I explained that women are attracted to men who can get things done.

Well, part of getting things done is learning how to do those things and in order to do that, you need to search out answers and change according to what you learn. Changing an opinion or approach is a sign of intelligence, not weakness.

If a doctor makes a diagnosis but then gets more information and realizes the diagnosis was incorrect, he's not going to continue with the initial decision. He is going to change based on the new information. The sign of a good doctor is one who can adjust to new evidence.

Change is good. Try new things. Test them out and decide if you like them or believe in them.

Toxic Masculinity

Toxic masculinity is a term that has entered our language in the last few years and has become incredibly controversial.

In short, it is when a man shows stereotypically masculine traits that are taken to extremes. Often the phrase "boys will be boys" is a target, saying that male behavior is given an excuse no matter how damaging or offensive it might be.

Often, it is connected to male entitlement and the idea that men are deserving of certain things or positions simply because they are guys.

Now, I am not saying this doesn't happen because it most definitely does. How many times have you gone into a club or a bar and seen a guy who felt entitled to do what they want? They drank the night away, getting loud and demeaning to every-one, and demanded that women hang out with them and even go home with them. However, as men, we don't have to fall into this trap. You can be masculine without being "toxic."

It comes down to respect and responsibility. If we respect women and understand that they are equals in every way, the concept of toxic mascu-linity can be eradicated.

Now, being equal doesn't mean that we operate the same way. Women and men look for different things in life, especially when they are meeting new people of the opposite sex.

If together, as men, we pass on lessons of respect toward women and other people to the next gen-eration, we can all get along a little bit better.

Chapter 4: What Women Want

I've always heard that women are really compli-
cated to figure out. I have to disagree.

I think you need to start with the fact that every
woman is different and you need to embrace that,
but I've learned in my experiences with them
what they want when talking to men.

The Top Ten Qualities Women Say They Look for in a Man

1. **Confidence**

2. **Sense of humor**

3. **Reliability and honesty**

4. **Not a pushover**

5. **Intelligence**

6. **Resourcefulness**

7. **Passion**

8. **Ability to communicate**

9. **A protector**

10. **Physicality/attractiveness and sex appeal**

So, let's break these down.

Confidence

It just keeps coming back to this, doesn't it?

Women love confidence. It's sexy and pulls them in. Remember, there is a difference between confidence and cockiness. Confidence is often unspoken, more of a vibe than the actual words. It's in the way you stand and the way you speak. And women can't get enough of it.

Sense of Humor

Having a sense of humor isn't just about telling a joke but also about not taking yourself too seriously. If you tease her, she's probably going to tease you back. In fact, you should hope she does because that's a sign she's flirting back and interested. So, don't get easily offended.

It's one thing to let a joke slide off you, but if you actually got insulted by a legitimate insult, make sure you don't get angry and just let it go. Although, it might be time to walk away. Remember your self-worth. You never should stand somewhere and allow someone to insult you.

Many times, the woman won't even realize that she said something that offended you. Just like men, women will sometimes gest without meaning any harm. When you point it out to them, they will apologize and back off. Often, this shows that you are willing to stand up for yourself without having to fly off the rails, and she will give you more respect. But if the woman tries to brush off your concerns or acts indignant for being called out on it, then you need to walk away.

Reliability and Honesty

Women don't like liars. It doesn't matter if you lied to them about cheating, what you do for a living, or that you are wearing clean socks. They want to know that you are telling them the truth.

They also want to feel that you are reliable. From the first time they meet you through dating and even into marriage, they want to know that you will be there for them and do what they ask and that you promise.

The classic example of this is the "Honey Do" list. When you are in a relationship, there will be things that she asks you to do, from errands to household things, and a lot of times couples call it the "Honeydew" or "Honey Do" list.

Some boyfriends and husbands don't take this list seriously, but it's a way to show that you are dependable. Make sure you are constantly checking things off and getting them done. Believe me, she notices.

Not a Pushover

You don't have to be over-demanding by any means, but you need to stand up for yourself. Don't let people (or her) walk all over you. While you want to do things for her, you aren't at her beck and call. You have a life and goals of your own.

Intelligence

Once, a woman was telling me about a guy she dated who was extremely handsome but not too smart. She told me a story about how once they were watching television and "bookends" were mentioned in a joke. Her boyfriend just looked at her, not understanding. She proceeded for ten minutes to try to explain to him what bookends were. He still had no idea. She finally got up, went to a shelf, and grabbed a pair and showed them to him. He laughed and said he didn't know they had names.

To make it worse, one day he was looking at the spices in her cabinet and started asking what things were while he mispronounced them. The woman told me that at that point, she knew the relationship was doomed. She would even tell the guy, "It's a good thing you're handsome." And he still didn't understand she was insulting him.

Women want you to have a brain in your head. You don't need to be a rocket scientist, but you need to know how the world works and how you fit in. And always learn how to pronounce the names of spices.

Resourcefulness

Women love a guy who can figure stuff out without sweating. It can be something as small as changing out a broken light bulb with a potato (look it up!) or finding a way to get tickets to a sold-out concert.

Women love that you can figure it out, especially when you have the ability to figure it out for them. It makes them feel special.

Passion

Women want a man who is passionate about things, and they know when you are serious.

It needs to be passionate about important things. First of all, they want you to be passionate about them, but they want to see it in the way you talk about work, family, and even hobbies.

Be forewarned, though, if your hobby is volunteering, she's going to be more impressed than the passion you express when, say, you gush over your baseball hat collection.

Ability to Communicate

Women want a man who knows what he wants and can put it into concise words. It doesn't matter if you are ordering a sandwich or talking to her about a relationship.

Women are constantly complaining that men don't open up to them. This is a bit misleading to men. They think that women want them to open up the floodgates and let emotions and feelings out.

Now, you don't need to bottle up everything, but they aren't looking for an hour-long session of telling her your innermost thoughts and feelings. She really just wants you to be honest and tell her things.

As men, all too often we are taught to bottle things up and carry on. Many men are told to hide their emotions and to bottle them up. They think that they shouldn't show off their emotions. But how can that help when you are trying to relate to another person?

Be honest. If there is something bothering you, tell her. If there is something in the relationship you aren't getting (even sexually), tell her. How is she going to know if you don't tell her?

A Protector

Women want to feel safe. You don't even have to do anything but let them know you are there for them.

It's going to be different with different women, too. I need to mention here that I am pretty tall. Once upon a time, I dated a woman named Lauren who was a former model and about 5'10". I also dated another woman named Kate who was about 5'5." They each wanted to feel protected, but in different ways.

Kate loved the feeling that I was so much bigger, she could get lost in my arms when I wrapped them around her. She would tell me how secure it made her feel and that when she was with me, she felt safe.

Lauren, on the other hand, didn't need to feel physically protected in the same way because she was so much taller. Heck, she was taller than a lot of guys out there. But she told me she felt safe as well for different reasons. She said she felt as though I had her back. That she could take care of herself, but just in case she didn't, she had me as a backup. She called us partners in crime.

Protection isn't always about being big and being able to physically sweep her away from danger. Sometimes it's more emotional and psychological.

Physicality/Attractiveness and Sex Appeal

Of course, she needs to be attracted to you physically, but did you know it can be a lot more than how you look that attracts her to you? It's actually a combination of all the above things.

True, some people just aren't going to be attractive to others, especially if you don't take care of yourself externally, but it's so much more.

By being her protector and making her feel safe and cared for, you are triggering primal urges in her brain. Going all the way back to the days of the cavemen, women are biologically wired to find the best mate. While part of that is physical attractiveness, their brains are wired to look for the man who can provide her with the best offspring, who can protect her against danger and other men, who will be trustworthy and always come home to take care of her.

So, when you show her that you offer these other things, it builds her attraction to you on a primal level.

Find Out What Interests Her

So, how do you show her how you fit into her categories?

Well, it's not just as simple as rattling down the list and telling her which things on her checklist you qualify for. She wants to know exactly how and she wants to discover it.

So, you need to do some work. You need to organically see how you fit in and then show her where you match and have connections. She needs to find out that you are the right guy, but you definitely need to help it along.

Ask Her Questions

During a conversation, women love it when you ask them questions. The problem is that a lot of guys don't know how to ask questions.

Make sure you ask real questions that will reveal something interesting about her and follow up.

Turning around from a Dead End

If you ask her something and the answer is a dead end, sometimes you can turn it naturally.

You may have just gotten back from a great vacation and have a good story to tell, but you ask her if she likes to travel and she says not really, you probably don't want to tell that story. So, what do you do? **Turn it.**

"So, you must do a lot locally. Any cool places I should know about?"

See, it's turning a negative into a positive and pushing the conversation forward.

Don't Go On...And On... And On.... And On....

If you are telling a story, don't go on for everything. Don't dominate the conversation. Conversations are about give-and-take and back-and-forth. If you are doing all the talking, she's going to get turned off.

Don't Be Cruel

Women like a little teasing, but everyone has their limits. Always be aware as you are finding that limit and don't fall into cruel or mean jokes.

They Want You to Listen

That woman you are talking with wants to feel like there is no one else in the room. Put that phone down, don't glance around, and give her your full attention.

It seems pretty simple, but all too often we don't give people the attention they deserve. Our minds might wander and what we don't realize is that our facial expressions change when we are not actively engaged in listening. People can tell, and you don't want a woman you are talking to realize she's basically talking to herself.

Mansplaining

This is a new term that is in society, but it's not a new act by any means.

Mansplaining is when a guy overexplains or simplifies something to a woman in a way that comes across as condescending or, often, incorrect.

One of the things I have learned over my experiences with women is to respect them. Don't try to assume they aren't as smart as you. Hey, I'm not saying there aren't some women who lack intelligence out there, but there are some pretty stupid dudes roaming the earth as well.

Men need to realize women will ask for help or an explanation if they need one. Many women today have advanced degrees and careers, and they are just fine figuring things out on their own. Unfortunately, it's still fairly common for men to feel the need to correct women, especially in STEM-related topics, even when they know that the woman has the same amount or more knowledge of a certain subject than they do. I've even seen men start out condescending while "explaining" something to a woman only to find out it's that woman's area of expertise—and then they doubled-down and refused to admit they were out of line or wrong.

Maybe it has something to do with feeling superior, but mansplaining isn't necessary. I remember talking to one of my friends who has spent a number of years working in a research and development capacity for a big company. She recounted so many stories of men who felt it was their job to explain every little detail of a specific situation to her, whether it had to do with the job or the latest football game.

While some women may need these things explained, it is never a good idea to assume. In fact, with this particular friend, she had a higher degree and understanding of the topic than the men who were trying to overexplain things to her, and she was able to point out several instances where the information they provided was wrong. Plus, as an avid football fan, she was able to hold her own there.

If the woman needs something explained, she will ask. Never assume that just because she is a woman, she won't understand what is going on.

So, especially in conversations, she doesn't want to hear you try to explain the workings of some machine. Even if she asks you a question about something you know a lot about, don't bore her or insult her by giving a lecture. Make sure that you don't talk down to the woman, either. It is fine to be passionate about something, but if you are lecturing the woman or she seems bored, then it is time to move on to a new topic.

Some men even try to mansplain a woman's own feelings to her. If that sounds absurd, that's because it is, but it also happens. Another female friend of mine told me a story about this happening to her while she was in college. She started going on dates with a young man from one of her classes, and a mutual male acquaintance of theirs started talking to her one day about how it was going. She wasn't sure she felt any chemistry with the guy and explained to the acquaintance that, for personal reasons, she didn't feel like he was the right person for her. The acquaintance then proceeded to tell her that she didn't think that she deserved love and went into a whole amateur psych evaluation for her. Needless to say, this made her uncomfortable, and she both stopped talking to the acquaintance and broke things off with the young man.

Long story short, don't be a jerk. Don't try to explain something to a woman who clearly has more knowledge of it than you do, especially when that "something" involves her own emotions. Just as importantly, make sure that your male friends don't mansplain things to women, especially one you want to talk to. It might bite you in the butt instead.

In the next section, we are going to the field. And if you like what you've learned so far, or you've found benefit, feel free to leave a review on Amazon. I really appreciate it as your feedback means a lot to me.

Part Two: In the Field

Chapter 5: Those First Few Words

You see her across the room. She's beautiful and exactly your type. You have the courage, you know what you are going to talk about, so you start across the floor-

WAIT!!!!

Hold on a second. Before you walk over, are you ready?

How You Present Yourself

In *How to Attract Women*, I extensively go into how to develop your own style, dress, and take care of your appearance. We also covered hygiene in *How to Flirt with Women*, but if not, make sure to check it out. They will help you immensely.

So, before you head out the door, ready to meet someone new, I offer a rundown of this quick checklist:

- Hair looks good?

- How's the breath?

- Are clothes straight?

- Fly isn't open?

- Know what you are going to say?

- How's your mindset? Is it positive and solid?

- Seriously, fly's not open, right?

Still not ready? Why?

Fear

It's possible that you want to walk over and feel ready but are still afraid.

So, what if you are afraid to go speak to a woman?

Well, first of all, it's normal. You're excited, you see a hot girl, your heart is pumping a bit.

Here's the short answer:

Conquer it.

That's what you have to do. Whether you have to just take a deep breath and take the plunge or mentally prepare yourself, you have to find a way to get over it.

What are the most common fears you might be experiencing?

What If She Says No?

Rejection sucks, it does. It doesn't matter if it's from a girl, a job, or from anywhere. We don't like to feel rejected.

But what if she does?

It's a few minutes out of your life. It's nothing personal. It's not that you are a bad person or that she thinks you are inferior in some way. It's just not right. There is nothing wrong with that.

If you did get rejected, think of it as practice. You tried some good conversation, some of it might have worked, other things might have fallen flat.

That's how human beings learn, from our failures. As we discussed earlier, part of being a fulfilled man is learning from things that went wrong.

Now the next time (maybe even in a few more minutes) you talk to a woman, you have a little more experience under your belt and knowledge of how to approach the situation.

What If She Has a Boyfriend or Is a Lesbian?

While they are both kinds of rejection, finding out that the woman has a partner and learning that she is a lesbian can cause their own special forms of embarrassment. Like with all rejection, don't take it personally. It really doesn't say anything about you. Her having a boyfriend does not mean that it's your fault for not getting there sooner, and her being a lesbian does not reflect on your masculinity at all.

If you want to hang around and talk with her just to be her friend, great, do it! Female friends are awesome. But if you're doing it with the thought that you might be able to change her mind about anything, get that out of your head right now. You won't, and if you come at a friendship with a woman with that mindset, she will find out and it will not end well for you.

The important thing is that you don't act like a jerk. If you pester her after she says she has a boyfriend or you act homophobic after you find out that she's a lesbian, it will bite you in the butt. Women talk to each other, and your name will spread around. Be nice and just leave things peacefully, though, and women will respect you for it.

What If She Laughs at Me or Insults Me?

The odds of this happening are really low. Most women aren't cruel. If they aren't interested, the majority of the time they are going to be polite or at least be civil.

If she does become mean and laugh at you, look at it as big help coming from her. **If that's her personality and style, did you really want to get to know her anyway?** Why waste your time having a discussion with someone you are very quickly going to realize isn't very nice? She actually did you a big favor.

What If I Come Off as Nervous, Anxious, or Overeager?

While the more confidence you can approach, the more successful you will be, you may still have a bit of nerves. That's ok. As long as you do your best and are nice, it's going to be ok. Most likely, as the conversation moves along, you will become more comfortable and less nervous.

And remember, women get nervous, too. She might get a little tongue-tied as you talk as well. That's a good sign! It means she's feeling the connection and is into you!

What If I Say Something Stupid?

Maybe you will, maybe you won't. The key is to not think about it. Go in with the confidence that you can talk to women and make a good impression and that is what will happen. If you do say something that you deem "stupid", don't worry too much about it. Odds are that she'll either laugh it off or not even realize it happened. If she does, just try and salvage the conversation as best you can.

If things end there, it's no big deal. Just brush it off as another learning experience.

What If She Isn't Interested in Me?

While it's probably not going to happen during your first conversation, it's something that happens. Put it out of your mind for now. She doesn't even know you yet.

She hasn't had a chance to decide, so you need to introduce yourself so she can see how much more than a friend you can be.

What If She Thinks I'm a Creep?

There's one easy way to avoid this... don't be a creep.

Don't do anything that gives her reason to assume you are a creep or a player. There will be times when you will be found guilty before you even open your mouth and need to prove your innocence, but if you smile, are pleasant, and don't say anything crude, you'll be able to prove it pretty fast.

Is It a Good Time to Talk to a Woman?

One thing a lot of guys have a problem with is when to approach a woman. They don't look for the signs before walking up. It doesn't mean you shouldn't do it; it just means you need to find the right moment.

When She's on Her Phone

Obviously, don't walk up and interrupt her while she's making a phone call, but if she is actively texting, it's not a great time, either.

You don't want to interrupt her because one of two things is going to happen. She is either going to:

- Ask you to wait while she finishes the text, which gives her the power over you and can put you off balance

Or

- She's going to stop what she's doing and look up, annoyed, and also be thinking of what she was in the middle of when you interrupted her.

Neither of them is a good option, huh?

So, wait. It might take a minute, heck, there might even be a couple of false starts, but talk to her while her eyes aren't on that phone.

When She's Already in a Deep Conversation

I had this friend in college named Randall. Randall was a really nice guy, but he was the type of guy that girls thought of as a friend and he always had a hard time in social situations.

One thing that Randall used to do when he saw a girl he was interested in who was already in a conversation would be that he walked up and joined them. He would just start listening to the conversation and then join in.

He was a very smart guy and knew a lot, so he always had an opinion. But what would always happen would be the woman he was interested in would end up walking away and Randall was now stuck talking to the other people he was in this conversation with. He would miss out every time! Other times, it just came across as rude.

Sometimes he would be able to catch up with her and talk, but it still didn't work. He had already set himself in the not-interested column for that girl and it was too late.

Approach them one-on-one or at least when they aren't in deep conversation with others. If you do join in the conversation, steer it toward her and then find a way to peel her off from the group. Don't let her walk away on her own. If she does, join her.

If Randall had learned that lesson, he would have had much better luck.

When Her Body Is Already Saying "No"

Sometimes, a woman really doesn't want to be bothered but it's not evident why. She isn't talking with anyone, she's not on her phone, and she should, seemingly, be open to approach. But even if the circumstances are telling you it's a good time, her body language might be screaming at you that it's not.

Is she avoiding eye contact with everyone? Is she sitting at the bar with her back to the rest of the club-goers? Slouching? Rubbing her eyes? Any of these could be an indicator that she's upset about something, tired from a long day, reluctantly spending a night out when she wanted to stay in, or any other feeling that says, loud and clear, "Don't talk to me." You might think that you can cheer her up, but odds are, you'll just get ignored at best, maybe even slapped.

Somewhere She Doesn't Feel Safe

If you see a woman walking down a dark street at night, it's probably not the best time and place to strike up a conversation. She is not going to be re-laxed and approachable and, honestly, she might just mace you.

Judgment Calls

There are times when you are going to have to decide whether it's a good time or not to approach her. Most of the time, I would probably tell you, go for it. Nothing to lose, but you may have to lay on a little more charm.

The Gym

It is really tough to meet women at the gym. Now, I don't mean tough like it can't happen, it just has to be done carefully.

Women get hit on **ALL THE TIME** at the gym. I see it every time I am there. And what I have learned is if they are in the mood to talk to people, they'll let you know.

Remember that while most women put on makeup and try to look good when they go to the gym, it doesn't mean that they feel like it. They're sweating, they're straining, they don't really want to have a conversation or have someone judge them, so they really have to be interested and want to talk to you.

I have a thing I call "The Knowing Look." Let me explain how it works.

There's always some guy at the gym that is show-ing off or doing an exercise wrong or generally calling attention to themselves. At my gym, there is this one guy who is always having business calls while he is working out. He yells at employees while he half-heartedly does workouts around the gym.

When there is a woman near me that I find attrac-tive and this guy (or any person) is nearby, I'll catch her eye, give a slight shake of my head, and look at him and back to her. They'll laugh or nod their head in agreement, but we made a connec-tion. I might talk to her after the guy leaves or keep building on it depending on my mood or how cute she is.

Another pretty good rule of thumb, if those ear-buds are in or her hood is up, she doesn't want to be bothered. That's a universal "Do Not Disturb" signal.

Work

In *How to Flirt with Women,* I talked a bit about flirting with bartenders, waitresses, and flight attendants. Some of the rules are the same for flirting with any woman while she is working.

Remember that her boss is there, she is earning money and right now, that is way more important than you. So, you need to judge the situation to see if it's the right time to strike up a conversation.

If it's your barista and the coffee shop is full, probably not a good time. If things are dead and you are the only customer in the place, it's actually a good time to have a quick talk, at least enough to get her number.

If it's someone that you see on a regular basis but you only have a moment to strike up a conversation with them, maybe offer out a question that they can consider until the next time they see you. After a few back-and-forths, you could make the next question, "What is your phone number?" She might even beat you to it.

You also want to be careful if you flirt with someone at your own work. Make sure not to monopolize their time. Keep it brief and fun. You don't want to get them or yourself in trouble.

Funerals

Honestly, there's no reason why not. However, I would highly suggest don't try to chat up the daughter of the deceased or the like. Be respectful, and it might just be the time to lay some ground-work for the future.

Just make sure to watch your timing, what you say, and who is around. You don't want to be standing next to the grieving widow while you are setting up plans to go dancing.

Have a Plan Before You Walk Up

You may not know exactly how the conversation is going to go, but make sure you have a plan before you walk up. Do you know what you are going to start with? Are you going to comment on her or the location? Is your goal to get her number, ask her out?

You don't have to lock everything down, and you need to be able to improvise or change your plan depending on how it goes and the information you receive, but having a basic plan and maybe a backup is vital before you head over.

Why Pick-up Lines Don't Work

The only way pick-up lines work is if they are done as a joke, and even then, there are much better ways of approaching a woman. There's a mindset that goes against everything that I've laid out in this book and my others. You are telling yourself that you need some silly line to meet a woman instead of the genuine person that you are.

One of the things that I've covered is also that women like a man they can trust. So, if you have created some line and are trying to pass it off as who you are, you have just set yourself as a liar and lost her trust before she even knows it.

You will always get further with a true human connection. Trying to use a gimmick line is just a way to create an illusion of confidence and women will eventually see through that.

Striking up a Conversation

So, let's say there is a woman that you want to talk to at a store. What do you say?

Well, at that moment, there are three basic categories:

- You can talk about you, which could come off as a bit egotistical.

- You can talk about her, which could come off a bit creepy.

- Or you could talk about where you are, which is a common thing that connects you.

I usually go to the location. If it's at a store, I try to find something we have in common. At the grocery store, I might comment that I've tried the item they are looking at.

You can also talk about her, but it's kind of risky. If you stop a random woman in a store and tell her you think she has great hair, it's probably not going to go well.

Look for something that you can comment on to strike up a conversation. If you're behind her in line at a grocery store and she's checking out the cover of the tabloids, ask her if she thinks the story is real. It's a great conversation starter.

Make note of something pleasant where you are and mention it to her. There's always something positive and it's up to you to find it.

Asking for Help

Try to find something she might have the answer for. If you are at an event, ask if she knows where a specific room or event is. A little advice: don't ask for the bathroom. You don't want to put certain thoughts of what you do behind closed doors in her head.

Ask Her Opinion

Ask her what she thinks about something. If you are at the grocery store and she is looking at the same item you are, ask her thoughts on it.

If it's someone you know of but have never met, think if there is anything you have in common. Maybe friends or co-workers. You can always say, "We should probably meet, I'm John's friend…"

The Way You Speak

When people get nervous, it's normal to speed up their speech a bit and stammer. However, even if it's normal, you don't want to do this.

Concentrate on speaking slowly and distinctly. Push through. As you start talking back and forth in the conversation, it will go away.

So Where Can You Strike up a Conversation?

Ready for the answer? **Anywhere!**

Next chapter.

Ok, I'm kidding. It's true, though. You can meet and talk with women anywhere. You just have to learn to take advantage of the situation and location.

The Obvious

Bars and Clubs

It's a great way to meet women and talk, and alcohol helps. Depending on the type of bar or club and the music level, it might be tough. Plus, if you are looking for a specific type of woman, this might not always be the best place to find them.

Also remember that, like at the gym, women get hit on all the time at bars and clubs. Some women are even scared going anywhere in these places alone because some men get so aggressive with their approaches, so be aware that they will be traveling at least in pairs.

School

This is a really obvious one because most of us probably met our first girlfriends in middle or high school or at least interacted with girls. This is one of the greatest places to have conversations with women because they are usually age-appropriate and have similar experiences at the institution.

Schools are also great because of the large number of social activities often connected to attending: sporting events, social events, parties, outings, and clubs. There are many activities that can help create a common interest and open up opportunities to meet women.

Even the classes themselves can be a great place to strike up a conversation. Just remember that at the collegiate level, most people are more serious about their academics, so choose when and what you talk about carefully.

Consider this scenario: you arrive to class about ten minutes before class. There's a test today, but you feel well prepared. Standing next to you in the hallway is a very pretty young woman with her nose buried in her notes for this class. You decide to start a conversation and try to talk to her about the upcoming test. You ask her if she's nervous, if she thinks it'll be hard, if she feels prepared, but all you're getting are one-word answers, nods, and the occasional glare. By the time you enter the classroom, she wants nothing to do with you and sits as far from you as possible.

Now, let's change this and assume that you didn't bother her before class. You get through the test and are allowed to go as soon as you are done. Right behind you, the pretty woman leaves the classroom. She is not distracted by her notes, phone, or anything else, so you approach her and ask her what she got on a certain question. She looks at you and gives her answer—which is almost the opposite of the one you chose—and you joke about how you got that way wrong. You laugh and the conversation continues outside the building, ending in you exchanging phone numbers so that you can arrange a study session.

Outside of the aforementioned social events, meeting women at school can be very tricky. However, if you know how to time your approach, you can have success even around class time.

Meet-Ups

If you have a hard time meeting women in other places or are very busy with work, these can be a great way to meet them.

Even a situation like speed dating could be good if you have a hard time having conversations because it is going to force you to practice talking quickly. It will help you with honing your presentation of who you are, your quickest jokes, and stories.

The Not so Obvious

Fitness Class

This is different than the gym. Since you went through the bonding experience of the class together, you have something to talk about and share. Just be careful because sometimes women are a bit reluctant and feel a bit vulnerable when they don't think they look their best. Personally, I think women are incredibly sexy when they are working out.

Dance Class

I'm serious. Think about it. First of all, women love a man who knows how to dance. Plus, it will help you learn to move, which can come in great when touching a woman. Imagine when you bust out those impressive dance steps at the next wedding you attend.

Quite often there are more women than men in the class, so you are bound to be a valuable commodity when it comes the time to partner up.

If you have two left feet, don't worry. For one thing, the classes will help you get better at dancing. You might never win *Dancing with the Stars* or *So You Think You Can Dance*, but you'll learn at least a few moves. In the meantime, you can use your clumsiness to good-naturedly poke fun at yourself. You might just get some laughs and some offers for extra "help".

Throw a Party

Call everyone you know, invite them and tell them to bring all their friends and all the girls they know.

When I was in college, we came up with an idea. We went to the local liquor store and got a huge Mexican beer poster. Then we hung it on the wall backwards so that it was just a blank white sheet.

During every party, we had people write their name and number and we would contact them for the next party. Next time, more would sign. And the next party and the next. Two years later, the poster was covered with the names of people. So, when we wanted to call a certain girl, we had their number.

Words Have Value

Mark Twain famously wrote, *"It's better to keep your mouth shut and appear stupid than open it and remove all doubt."*

This is very important and true when interacting with not only women but in life in general.

I see it all the time. Men are trying to impress a woman and rambling on about topics to the point where they are repeating themselves or trying to fill in the information they don't have by creating stories (otherwise known as lies).

It's a horrible thing to do because it's nobody's fault but your own. Sometimes it's just better to listen and keep your mouth closed.

Chapter 6: Connecting and Chemistry

It doesn't matter how much effort you put into talking with a woman. If you don't have some sort of connection or chemistry, it's not going to move forward.

As I've said before, sometimes it's instant before you even utter a word, but that's not always going to happen. However, you can do things to make the attraction and connection stronger from the first moment she sees you.

Making an Instant Connection

There are several ways you can make sure you connect with someone. It's about making them feel comfortable with you, as if you have a history. In order to do that, make sure you incorporate these points early in your conversation:

Listen

When people know they are being heard, they are more likely to feel connected to you. It's universal. Everyone wants to feel important. So, when you acknowledge that you are listening and comprehending what she is saying, that bonds her to you, helping create a quick and strong connection.

Make a Strong First Impression

When you first speak to her, make sure you come across as well as possible. Stand up straight, speak clearly, and, of course, smile. The more confident you are, the more of an impression you will make.

Don't Stay in the Shallow End

Always remember that this woman probably gets hit on a dozen times a day and most of the men who do it have no idea what they are doing. You need to differentiate yourself, which is easy because you do know what you are doing.

Don't be superficial. Don't fall into small talk or cheesy lines. Be real. Go right into the interesting conversation and she's going to be impressed and connected.

Be Intelligently Inquisitive

Ask brief, good questions that she can answer so she can share information about herself. Make sure to offer smart follow-up questions that continue to push the conversation forward.

Make sure you don't turn the conversation around to you. Too many men tend to take the small amount of information they just got and relate it to their own experiences. This will alienate her incredibly quickly.

Learn from Her

If she tells you something you didn't know about a topic, acknowledge it. Tell her that you didn't know that and that you learned something. Thank her. This will cause a connection.

Call Her by Name

You got her name, right? By using her name naturally, it creates a connection. Don't overuse it, though. That can come across a bit creepy. Just use it when it's natural in the conversation.

Make Your Comments Genuine

Don't just fill the conversation with generic statements and rehearsed comments. Be genuine about what you talk about and your interests. She's going to be able to tell unless you are an incredibly good actor. If you aren't genuine and it works out, it will come back to haunt you.

Don't Play the One-Up Game...

I dated a woman once who, when I would tell her about something bad that had happened, would always immediately tell me back something else in her life that was just that bad or worse.

I finally asked her about it (not long before we stopped dating) and told her that I felt as if she wasn't listening to me. She said she absolutely was, it was her way of sharing the bad and commiserating with me.

That's not the way to have a conversation. If someone is opening up to you with something that is a bit personal, they are trusting you. By throwing out your own story, it tells them that you aren't being affected by what they are saying. So, listen, ask some questions, maybe steer the conversation to other topics if it was a tough story.

...Unless You Know How to Do It

Now that I've said that, there are times to do it when it will impress her. However, never when it's a negative.

I get to travel to a lot of countries for work, so I usually have some fun stories about far-off places. So, if I am having a conversation with a woman and we are talking about travel, I will let her tell me her favorite story first. Usually, it's a story about traveling somewhere cool but not necessarily exotic or even international.

I will show complete interest and then offhandedly mention that's better than the weird places I have to travel to and ask another question about her story but a very superficial one. Usually, she'll answer it but be interested in why I said weird places. I'll comment and say that I usually end up in places like Russia, Asia, or South America for work. Most of the time, she'll forget about her travel stories and want to hear about where I have visited.

The idea is to make her want to know more about you but not force it on her or try to one-up her. You just have to play it smooth.

Perceived Humility vs. Putting Yourself Down

There are some guys who use a whole put-down style when they talk to girls. They think that by putting themselves down, the woman will think they are humble and start to see the good things in them as they counteract the bad comments. They hope the conversation will go something like this:

She: *I really like your hair.*

He: *Really? I've never liked it. The color. I wish I could change it. I hate it.*

This doesn't work. It's going to do one of two things. Either she is going to perceive it as a lack of confidence and shut you down or she is going to feel sorry for you and build you up, but she'll do it as your new friend.

Be humble about yourself, but it's ok to be proud. Never put yourself down. You might state that there's room for improvement in a certain area, but don't make yourself sound like a loser by complaining about what you don't like about yourself.

Saying "I'm Sorry"

I grew up saying I was sorry. I was taught that it was the proper thing to do. To me, it was accepting responsibility for what you did and apologize. It seemed right.

But as I grew older, I started to hear from women they hated it when guys were always apologizing. I didn't understand. I thought that's what women wanted, for a man to admit they were wrong! I mean, we joke about it in society so much that entire sitcoms are created around the husband constantly apologizing.

Then, when I was in my freshman year of college, I met this cute girl and flirted with her badly but enough to strike up a conversation. I apologized for something and for the first time, she explained to me why women hated it. It has always stuck with me.

You apologize when you have wronged someone purposefully or through malice or lack of attention. It has to be of a certain degree of pain or loss inflicted. We use "sorry" too easily in modern society. We apologize for things we haven't done, saying, "I'm sorry." We use the same words for accidentally putting our coat on someone's chair as we do when we have physically hurt someone causing great pain.

So, when you are tempted to say sorry for not a very good reason, try something else. I personally tend to look at something and say to the person, "That's no good. Let's fix that." Or something similar.

Don't come across as overly apologetic. To a woman, this is going to sound insecure and a lack of confidence. Of course, this is something that women do as well. Everyone can feel a bit nervous, and the frequent "sorry's" that follow can make you feel even worse. Work on your confidence, and this will get better.

How to Help Chemistry Get Along

Now, I'm going to be honest with you. Yes, you can talk to any woman and these books are going to give you all the skills you need. However, the fact is there will be women who just don't want to talk to you. It might not even be your fault. It might be they are busy, mentally just not interested in talking, or their mind is on something else.

There will be times when no matter what you do, the chemistry just isn't there. Don't feel bad. It happens to everyone, even me. It's not a loss or something you did wrong.

However, other times the chemistry is there, it's just buried a bit or turned off. It's up to you to get things moving.

There are things that you can do to give the chemistry a bit of a push:

- Make sure the conversation is balanced. Don't dominate it, but don't be silent, either. Keep a good back-and-forth by asking questions and offering information on yourself.

- Be positive! Don't dwell on negative things or relay negative stories and thoughts. Keep it light and fun!

- Make sure you are talking in a location where you can have a conversation. Don't try to have a conversation in a dance club next to the speaker or standing outside in the cold while she's shivering. Have conversations in places where it's comfortable and both of you will feel like staying and chatting for a while.

- Don't bring up past relationships. It's okay to mention an ex, but don't dwell on it. She doesn't want to hear about all the bad dating experiences you had. If you keep going on about your ex, she's going to think you aren't over her. You might bond over bad date stories, but don't stay on the topic forever.

- Get her thinking. Ask her questions and "what ifs?" It'll get her brain going and can move the conversation into stimulating territory. She wants to talk with someone who will make the conversation memorable.

- Make her laugh. Everybody loves to laugh. Humor is a great unifier. If you can make her laugh and figure out your sense of humor, it will do wonders for creating a connection between you.

Share through the Senses

Experiences are important to having a connection. However, you don't have to do things in order to make a connection.

Use your senses to share experiences. Try each other's food (with permission, of course). By both sharing the same sensory experience with taste, you now have a connection that only the two of you have. That's a great way to get closer.

Music works as well. If you can find a common connection of a favorite song, the deeper chemistry will bond you over music. Never underestimate the power of good music.

Share Your Fantasies

Now, it doesn't need to be that fantasy you had about your sexy homeroom teacher when you were in high school. It doesn't have to be sexual at all. It can be more about your fantasies in life. Where you would like to visit, what you would like to do and accomplish.

However, if you can steer the conversation to sexual fantasies without going too far, it's a great way to get her to open up and trust you, as long as you reciprocate and tell her yours.

Touch

I have talked about touching in this book as well as in *How to Flirt with Women* and *How to Attract Women*, but I will continue to talk about it because it is unbelievably important.

Humans are social creatures. We crave attention and affection and part of that is human contact. If you can make safe, pleasurable contact with her, it will create a bond.

Again, though, I cannot stress enough, make sure it's proper contact. Touching her inappropriately will end the conversation quicker than you can imagine. You have to take your cues from the woman, but touching them lightly on the arm, at the small of the back to lead them, and other similar touches can help you to create a sense of intimacy with them.

Trust

One of the most important parts of making a connection with a woman is trust. Not just physical trust that you aren't going to hurt her or turn out to be a creep, but trust that you are listening and being honest. And that you aren't just looking for sex.

I know what you are thinking. "Wait... what... but I thought..."

Look, she knows you are trying to get laid. Everybody wants to get laid, even her. But what she wants to know is that she isn't just a number and that you've already started looking at her as something you conquered.

Even if it's only going to be a one-night stand, she wants to make sure she gets out without being hurt and that everyone was honest.

Let Her Know You Are Interested

This one seems pretty simple, but so many guys get it wrong. I hear it from many of my female friends. They were talking to a guy and he was very casual and the conversation went nowhere. They thought he was cute, but they didn't know that the guy was even interested in them.

Make sure to drop some comments so she knows you are into her. Don't say something stupid or too forward. Play it cool. Give her a wink and say something like "You know, you're pretty cool." It's all in the delivery, as if you had a revelation.

Act Protective

This doesn't mean mark your territory. It means do things that let her feel important and protected. Help her off with her coat and throw a little chivalry her way. Show her you care, but don't go too far.

Be in the Moment

Talking about the past or your history or things that already happened are not great ways to make her closer. Be in the moment, talk about whatever is going on between you right then. Don't move the conversation back in time to something you already discussed.

Give It Time

Some women just take longer to make a good connection. Maybe they are a bit protective in their personality, or maybe they have had bad relationships in the past and it takes a little more for them to open up.

It's not a big deal! If you like this woman and are interested in getting to know her, then give it a little time. Go on a few dates and let the connection grow.

However, if you are getting to the third or fourth date and it's all conversation and no connection, it might be time to move on.

Ask Her Opinion

Try asking her opinion about something. It can be small or something a bit larger or more important. It really depends on where you are in your conversation and what type of woman she is.

Make sure it's because of other actual intelligence. If she is a doctor or a lawyer, don't go fishing for free professional advice. Ask her opinion on a current event or something else in the news to get her insight.

By valuing her opinion, this will help turn up the chemistry between you and continue to deepen your connection.

Make a Fun Bet

By making a playful wager, it's going to take your conversation to another level. Make sure the winner gets something fun. Maybe the loser has to tell an embarrassing story, or the winner gets a kiss is always a good one. Even if you are on a date, it's still a fun game to play.

Secrets

A great way to make a connection with a woman that you are talking with is to create a bond through secrets.

What you are doing is creating your own little world with this woman. By creating secrets that you share, you make steps toward making a connection that no one else shares with her but you.

There are several ways that you can go about this. One way I use a lot to great success is to play a sort of "I Spy" with the room.

While you are talking, spot someone in the room doing something silly and funny. Tell her not to look right at them but start to talk about the person. Turn it into a game, finally telling them to look.

One that works really well for me is to find a guy who looks like he is hitting on a girl with no success. Together, you and the woman you are talking with can begin your own running commentary. It's fun and also a way to move the conversation to yourselves. You can casually make a comment that you hope you are doing better than that guy. If you are, she'll let you know at this point.

People Watching

Have you ever sat on a park bench, watched people go by, and made a mental narrative about the ones who have caught your eye? Then you've played the people-watching game. It's a fun pastime when you're alone, but it's even more fun when you do it with someone else. Why not do that with a woman you're interested in?

One time, I went to get a drink with a couple of coworkers to unwind after a particularly long work week. When we got there, we took seats at the bar, and I sat next to a woman who seemed to be there with a couple friends. At one point, we struck up a conversation over us both drinking Long Island Iced Teas. The conversation started to lull, so I swiveled on my stool and started watching the crowd. In came a group of men and women who looked like they had just walked off the set of *Mad Men*. I leaned over to the woman I had been talking to and asked, "Hey, what do you think their deal is?"

She turned around and laughed, and we both started providing our theories about these oddly dressed people, everything from a themed wedding to time travelers who were accidentally brought here by the Doc. It was so fun that my coworkers and her friends joined in, and soon we were all bursting with laughter. By the end of the night, I had the woman's number.

People watching is good fun and gives you a chance to get to know each other on a deeper level. You find out the kinds of things that pop into her mind on-the-fly, what makes her laugh, and how creative she is. It'll also show her how fun and imaginative you are.

Chapter 7: Having a Conversation

Having a conversation isn't difficult. We have them with dozens of people as we move through every day. But having a conversation with a woman you are interested in is going to be something different.

Topics

Topics are going to depend on two things: you and her. You need to learn what topics she's passionate about and how deeply she is interested in delving into them.

Personally, I am a big news junkie. I read the news all day long and will often follow stories as they develop. I like to be on top of everything.

Now, some women I talk with love to keep up on the news as well, while others barely know where to find Washington, D.C., on a map. But that's fine. That just means I gauge the conversation.

Sometimes, I'll be ready for a heavy political discussion with a woman, while other times, it's just a simple current event headline that she found interesting, but not because she wanted to know, it's because I knew it and she was impressed at my knowledge. Or I'll steer to something else altogether.

Usually, there are certain topics that are safe to pursue until you learn a bit more about the woman:

Pets

She doesn't have to have pets of her own because odds are she had at least one pet growing up that was her favorite. If you both share having pets currently, it opens up the whole world of topics, especially if they are the same, such as you both have dogs.

But if one of you is a cat person and one of you is a dog person, fret not. It's actually a great opportunity to have a fun debate about which is better. While you should never give in that her way is better, don't be mean or cruel. Just be playful and tease her a bit, but the fact is that you both love animals, so nobody is wrong.

Travel

Most people enjoy traveling or at least the destination once you arrive. She may not have been around the world (or maybe she has) but most likely, she wants to travel more, just like most people.

Ask about where she has been and where she wants to go. What is her favorite place she's ever been? Or what is the one place that she hasn't been but wants to?

Be prepared, she's going to ask you the same question, so your answer better be something better than Spring Break in Florida.

Movies & Television

It's tough to find someone who doesn't have a favorite movie or television show, so it's a pretty safe topic. But don't just throw out the question, "Seen any good movies lately?"

Food

Everyone has a favorite food, even if it's just a burger and fries. We all like to eat. Talk about what types of cuisine she likes. Does she have a favorite restaurant? Is there a food she's always wanted to try but hasn't yet?

Be Specific

No matter which subject you go with, remember to be specific. Ask her what the last movie she enjoyed was or if there's a show she's currently binging. Move away from generics to more interesting conversations about deeper meanings in film or how they affected both of you. Just saying something looked cool because they had great special effects isn't going to be enough.

How to Talk to Her

What Kinds of Questions Should You Ask?

As you pose questions to her, you want to sound like you just thought of them. Also, when you ask questions, you don't want them to be ones that have to be thought out. Some people don't have a favorite movie or band and you are going to have to think and it gets distracting. Ask ones most people can answer quickly. This could include what is their favorite color, where they would like to travel, what books they have read recently, and more.

Follow-ups

So, you just asked her where she grew up. "Boston." Now you have a decision to make.

You can say "Cool" and then tell her where you grew up. Then you'll find something else to talk about.

I have a better idea. Respond to the information you just got. Talk about her hometown. Follow up with a question about: "Was it fun", "Do you go back", "Do you like it?"

If she doesn't really want to talk to you about it, she may ask you about your hometown. This makes her interested in you, plus you just learned that hometown memories might not be a great topic.

- **Ask her about her free time**

    Does she read? What was the last book she got into? Sports? Hobbies? Other interests?

- **What's the last bad movie you saw?**

  It's a little different and shows you have a sense of humor.

- **What's your guilty pleasure?**

  Everyone has that movie, TV show, magazine, or maybe a sweet thing that they love to enjoy. Ask! Plus, a side note, getting the "guilty" in there is a bit of an innuendo.

- **What is your least favorite household chore?**

  Everybody hates chores, it's a universal truth. So, you aren't going negative, and you two are sharing an experience.

- **So, what were you like when you were a kid?**

  This is a way to ask about her family indirectly. If you ask too much, she may not want to reveal it so soon or, worse, she might feel like it's intrusive. This way, she'll tell you some fun stuff without feeling threatened.

- **What is your biggest pet peeve?**

  Just like everyone hates chores, everyone has a pet peeve. It's just a fact of life. Usually, it's not even anything that is serious, hence the name "pet peeve". It's a playful way to dig deeper into the kind of person she is, and it could even open up an opportunity for some good-natured teasing. Just remember to not make fun of her too much for her pet peeve. And if you find yourself doing what she's named as her pet peeve, make a conscious effort to stop. She'll appreciate your consideration.

- **What was the best thing that happened to you today?**

  Great question because it puts her in a positive mood and is direct. You didn't ask the old "how was your day," you asked her to tell you something that she is excited about.

How to Listen

Look for the Commonalities

Look for the things the two of you have in common. Interests, where you grew up, where you went to school, or where you live in the city.

However, it doesn't mean you need to ignore the differences. You can find some great ways to talk about your unique takes on places and subjects.

Don't Agree with Everything Just to Be Nice

You want to find commonalities, but don't agree with things that aren't true. If she likes a certain band and you don't really care for them, don't act like you do, say you don't.

Maybe use it as a chance to tease her a little bit. Don't be a jerk about it, but it shows her you have a mind of your own.

"Are You Seeing Someone?"

When this is asked by the woman, this means that they are interested. They aren't looking for that information unless they want to know if it's worth moving forward.

Put Away that Phone

That phone doesn't need to be out unless you are showing her something or getting her numbers ("By the way, just saying... as long as it's out, why don't you give me your number.")

Eye Contact

Eye contact is always important, but especially when you are listening. Make sure that you are engaged.

If she is telling you a personal story with an emotional connection, the eye contact will help create a bond with you. But don't make it too intense and remember to blink and look away every now and then. Otherwise, the woman will grow uncomfortable and you might even creep her out.

Don't Respond until She's Finished

We all know it's not polite to interrupt, but many people have the habit of opening their mouth and getting ready to answer or add to the conversation before the other person is finished speaking.

Not only is this rude, but you are actually proving to them that you aren't actively listening at the moment. If you were, you wouldn't have a question ready to go unless they were finished. Sometimes people will even point a finger at the other person until they are done and they can launch into their own thoughts.

I had an ex-girlfriend who had her own version of this. I would be saying something to her and she would lock onto something I said in the first sentences and then be ready with a statement once I finished. I tried to explain to her that she wasn't listening to me because she was concentrating on holding that thought and not open to anything else I was saying.

So, don't become focused on something you need to say. Let them finish and if it's important enough, it will still be with you or will come up organically in your mind.

Don't Change the Subject

Never decide that you have a new topic that is better than what she was talking about. A good conversationalist can see places where they can expand topics or steer the conversation.

If you blatantly go in another direction after she says something, it's going to come across as extremely rude and won't end well.

Use Minimal Encouragers

Did you know that the noises, while you are listening to someone, had a name? Those little sounds you make are called minimal encouragers. These short verbal sounds actually encourage the person speaking to continue and elaborate.

They really do work in conversations because they aren't invasive and give the speaker the reassurance that you are present in the conversation.

Repeat Back What You Heard

There is a practice called active listening which, in simple terms, is just saying back what you said in a way that lets the speaker know that you heard them and that you are in the moment.

You don't want to sound like you are mimicking them, but just say enough that they know you understood. You might not want to implement this all the time, but if she is telling you something detailed or important, it's a way for you to know you understand and for her to know as well.

How to Keep the Conversation Going

I just talked about listening, which is a major portion of keeping the conversation fresh and moving forward. By listening, you can ask more questions and keep her engaged.

When she asks you questions, try to add tidbits about other stories. I might say, "...and it was probably the second-best time I've ever had in another country", which leaves her wanting to know what the first was. But don't offer it, make her ask and come to you.

A good conversation is like a really gripping movie. It moves along and you just want to know more and what's going to happen next. If you can create that same type of moment when you are talking with a girl, you are a complete success!

When to Let It End

There are times when you have no choice but to end talking to a woman through no fault of your own. You might be late for an appointment or she might have to go, even though you are completely engaged. If the conversation has been going well and you have been talking back and forth, it's the perfect reason to ask for her number. Right here and now.

If the conversation is coming to a natural end, you either have to try to start it back up or get her number. It might be time to just go for the digits.

Signs She's Not That into You

It happens to everyone, but it's not a bad thing, especially if you learn the signs and when is the right time to cut your losses.

Short Answers

One-word answers and a basic attitude of non-interest. If she is treating you the same way a bored grocery store clerk does, she's probably not that into you.

Vague Answers

If she doesn't answer questions, won't give you definitive answers, or almost seems like she is hiding something, she's looking for a way to get out of the conversation. Your charm might win her over eventually, but you need to decide how much time is worth it. You might miss another amazing opportunity while you keep trying with a woman who will be going nowhere.

She Ignores Your Texts and Messages

It's pretty simple that if she were into you and wanted to be with you, she would return your messages or texts. A little time is one thing, but if you haven't heard from her for days, she's getting them and not replying. It might be time to consider moving on.

Something Keeps Coming Up

Whether it's the first meet and she keeps getting distracted by friends or the phone or if you are trying to schedule a date and she keeps having things that come up and she reschedules or flakes out, you want someone who is excited to see you and talk to you. This ain't that girl.

She Lies to Your Face

This one is always fun. I've seen guys walk up to girls and offer to buy them a beer. They smile, say they don't drink, and then take a long swig of their own beer.

If they are just saying things to try to avoid you or be nice but negative, make sure you realize it. Some guys get so focused on what they are doing they don't notice these signs that she's not into you and trying to communicate that.

Body Language

I've talked a lot about how body language plays into flirting, attraction, and conversation. It's one of the first things you can tell as you talk with a woman whether or not she's into you. If she won't even turn toward you when you approach or is closed off with her arms across herself, she's not that into you. Even avoiding eye contact can be a sign that she's ready to move on.

Body language can change as the situation does, so you can get her to warm up. But if she stays that way or moves to it, you are not looking good.

Also remember that body language is informed by the situation, someone's culture, and the person. That's why you shouldn't jump to conclusions based on just one or two bad signs. Just proceed with caution and know when to walk away.

She Hints at It

Many people don't like conflict. If she feels that you like her and she doesn't reciprocate, she might try to preempt you with subtle or not-so-subtle hints. Most common is the "I have a boy-friend" line, but if she can't use that for some reason like she or a friend already told you she didn't, she'll try something else.

She might talk about how into her career she is or how much she has been enjoying "finding herself" being single. If she talks a lot about other men, it's also a pretty good sign she's not interested in adding you to the list.

If you ask her out, she might not want to give you a definitive answer, which is a real sign she's not interested. She either wants to or not, it shouldn't be something she needs to think about.

Hard to Get Vs. Get Away from Me

It is true that women play games, but then, so do we. Everybody plays their own games when they are dating and looking for love.

In *How to Flirt with Women*, I discussed the Push-Pull method that some men use to flirt and talk with women. In short, it's a way to pull them closer (emotionally and sometimes physically) before pushing them away. The idea is that the flux will cause the person to be more attracted to you.

Women have their own version that men usually refer to as "hard to get." In the old days, there was a joke that in dating certain women "Your lips say no, but your eyes say yes."

If you try this nowadays, you are going to ruin your life. If you are lucky, you'll get slapped. In a worst-case scenario, you could be arrested or socially ousted as a sexual predator.

However, women definitely play hard to get. They will make you work for their attention through conversation and proving you are worth their time. However, there is a difference between playing hard to get and just wanting you to go away.

Make sure you find the line. You don't want to give up too quickly because you might have misread some signs or she might just be playing a little too hard. But if she is really giving you the cold shoulder, has turned away, or maybe is even having a conversation with someone else, realize that it's not a good lead and it's time to move on.

If you are still getting teases and smiles, most likely, she's just playing hard to get. Just keep going for a bit and if she starts to warm up, you're in. If not, time to cut out.

Chapter 8: How to Steer a Conversation

It's really not that difficult to move a conversation to certain topics, we do it all the time. How often have you made small talk with someone at a bank or during a meeting before you got down to business?

It's the same principle with steering a conversation, but you want to make sure that the person whom you are talking with is going to be open to the new topic. Part of this is done through observation and listening and the rest is all in the presentation.

While it's obviously fun and sexy to talk about sex with a new woman, it's also a great way to learn if you do end up sleeping together. You might get a hint at her likes and dislikes and can implement them when the time is right.

Prime the Pump

Start using words that set the foundation for talking about sex.

Telling a woman she's sexy is more about a feeling than how she looks. You can tell her she's sexy and look at her in a way that she knows you're talking about the way she looks. She might take it as a compliment, but you can make it mean much more.

Tie it to something deeper. Her laugh, her sense of humor, the way she talks. This makes it much deeper and less superficial.

Talk About Love and Passion, Not About Sex

Women respond to mood and emotion, while men usually respond to visual cues. So, if you tell her how hot you thought a love scene in a movie was, she's probably not going to feel the same vibe.

However, if you told her you thought it was sensual and talked about the characters, she's going to be drawn in and be more open to discussing things of a sexual nature.

You don't want to come across as some horny teenager who saw a boob on the big screen. She wants a man, not a boy.

Innuendo

Innuendo is simply implying another meaning to a word that you say. When you make it a sexual innuendo, it's a lot more fun.

Try words like hard, come, wet, or moist. Phrases like "...slipped it inside...", "Things work better when they are wet", or "It's getting hard" work well.

You can also try to find ways to make a play on her employment. If she is a nurse, you could slip in a "naughty nurse" comment. Or maybe she's a schoolteacher and you could say something about her giving out discipline.

"I Had a Friend..."

Bring up a topic about someone else.

Tell her you have a female friend who had a sexual issue or story and tell her. Make sure to keep it simple so she doesn't ask details and suddenly you are stumped.

The fun of this is that you have just opened up a sexual conversation, but because it's someone else, she's going to feel more comfortable to speak freely. Also, you are asking her opinion, so you are adding to your deepening connection.

What If the Conversation Is Stalling?

You might run into resistance. She might not feel comfortable about sex, and after trying every approach, she's just not into the conversation.

It happens. Some people keep their sexuality very closed. It doesn't mean that she's not interested in sex. It's even possible she's such a sexual person that she has to keep it under locks.

If it's your first conversation and you can't steer it, that's ok. If it's your third date, maybe you should reconsider. This could be a sign that she isn't really that interested in you.

Not everyone is a sexual person. There are some women (albeit in my opinion the small minority) who aren't sexual and only need to have it once or twice a month. It really comes down to compatibility and what you are looking for. I discuss this at length in *How to Attract Women*.

Chapter 9: How to Get Past the Small Talk and Get Her Phone Number

You've been talking a few minutes and she seems like she's into you. But will she give you her phone number? Will she go out with you?

First of all, you need **to be in the mindset that of course she will.** She has given you no reason to think she wouldn't, so keep that positivity.

You have to believe that every woman you are interested in will give you her number. It's not arrogance. It's just a feeling of positivity and abundance. You are an intelligent, good-looking, and interesting guy, so there is no reason she would not want to get to know you. If you operate on this level, you will radiate confidence.

So, how do you move the conversation to a point where you can get her number?

Small Talk to Real Conversation

The biggest trick to moving from small talk and casual conversation to something more meaningful is to validate their interests and pull them into a deeper conversation.

All this means is to find the small things in what they are saying or doing that can be seen as important by both of you.

Let's try a hypothetical situation:

You are at a coffee shop and you notice a beautiful woman waiting for her coffee right next to you. You give her a smile, she smiles back and you have some good eye contact. She comments on your shirt color and you thank her.

Right as your coffee comes, you notice she has a nice bracelet that is very unique. You comment that it's really cool. She smiles, thanks you, and says she got it when she was traveling in Asia. You say that sounds cool and she smiles, says goodbye, and leaves.

What happened?

You had the perfect opportunity to turn casual small talk into a much deeper conversation. She gave you the perfect opening when she said she got her bracelet in Asia.

That's the opportunity to take a bit of small talk information and turn it into a conversation that is meaningful. Travel is a perfect opportunity. When people take a trip, especially to another country or part of the world, there is going to be an emotional connection. They are going to be happy to share.

If you had said something like "Asia? I've never been there. What was that trip like?", you would have opened up the door for a longer and more real conversation.

Look for those nuggets in small talk that can open women up.

Asking for the Digits

Before you ask, check yourself with a couple of things.

Check for that ring on her left hand. Make sure you didn't miss it. You don't want to realize you are hitting on a married woman. All good?

Did she say she's seeing someone? Some guys think that if she's got a boyfriend, she's still up for some fun. She's not married.

I think this is disrespectful and makes you less of a man. If you had a girlfriend and some guy tried to make a move, how would you react? It's one thing for her to say she has one, but if you know, back off. Treat her the same way you would want your own girlfriend treated.

Assume It's Going to Happen

Be confident that you two are going to go out and have fun. Don't say, "Is it ok if I ask you out?" You don't need permission to ask her. Just ask!

Be specific. Say, "Would you have dinner with me?" or "Maybe let's have dinner." Assume that she's just had a great conversation and of course she's going to want to see more of you! Come up with a day as soon as you can.

Snap a Picture

If you are somewhere interesting, offer to snap a photo and text it to her. You'll get her number. If getting her number doesn't seem right at the moment, offer to post it on Instagram and ask what her profile is and follow her. Then tag the photo and contact her online.

Use What You Have Learned

I will bet you that she has provided you with at least a dozen different ways to ask her out, but you didn't even realize it.

As she tells you things about herself, look for the information. What has she said she has wanted to do but never had the chance? You probably aren't in a position to take her to Paris, but if she said she's never had French food, ask her out to a French dinner. Does she want to see the new award-winning dramatic film coming out next week? Say you should go together.

During your conversation, you are getting to know her and the truth is she is telling you exactly what to do. She has told you her likes and dislikes, so you just need to figure out the best one for her right then.

Make sure it's one you can do right away. If she says she's excited about a movie coming out in six months, not a good idea to pursue that. You don't want to wait six months for a date. Or if there's a club or restaurant she's interested in but hasn't opened yet, don't wait. Find your opportunities!

Topics to Avoid

Your Exes

While it is common to find common ground with your past relationships, this can turn negative pretty quickly. Instead of having a positive experience and enjoying each other, you are going to bring up bad memories on both sides. Commiseration is not stimulating conversation that turns people on.

Personal Trauma

Unless you're talking to this woman at some sort of support group, try to avoid any discussion of past personal trauma until you've known her for a while. (And if you did meet her at such a group, remember to focus on healing first and being part of a support system for your fellow survivors, not getting laid by the cute girl by the snack table.) Trauma can be a real bonding agent and women want you to be open with them about your feelings—later in the relationship. Even mental health problems, something which we should always try to normalize so that people won't be afraid to seek help, should wait until you two are more comfortable with each other.

Until then, don't use this to propel a conversation, even if she provides you with the perfect opening. You don't want to scare her away.

TMI

You know that commercial where the woman is on a first date with this guy and when the guy mentions how awkward first dates can be, she replies, "Yeah, like my constipation"? You would hope that this commercial is just an exaggeration meant for comedic effect, but you'd be surprised. Some people really do share way too much in their first conversation with someone, especially if they get nervous or run out of things to say. Avoid this at all costs.

Obviously, bodily functions are off-limits. So is bragging about your sexual prowess or how hung you are. Like I said before, talk about love and passion, not sex. Besides, those organs are just not something women—or anyone—want to hear about when they first meet you. Gross.

Remember, use innuendo, but be subtle. Don't be TMI.

Politics and Religion

Eventually, this can become a wealth of conversation, but at first, be very careful bringing up politics and religion until you know where both of you stand.

Don't editorialize or go on about your personal beliefs, especially religion. If you go to church, say so but don't make her think you are highly religious and almost became a priest. If you aren't religious, don't lie and say you are, instead just touch on it saying you're not that religious. If it gets to the third and fourth date, then start talking about these things. But not yet.

Sports

She may love sports, but the vast majority of women don't want to talk about it all the time and definitely not the breakdown of box scores or how you can remember the entire line up of the 2016 World Champion Chicago Cubs baseball team.

She's probably going to ask if you watch sports and which ones. Tell her the truth, but don't dwell on it. She's trying to find out if it's such a dominating thing that it would potentially take away from the time you two might spend together.

Ask her if she watches or enjoys sports. Often women connect sports to emotional events, like family outings to games as a kid or watching football on Sundays with her dad.

You, however, most likely connect it to certain events, like the once-in-a-lifetime comeback you watched or an amazing play or the time a player got injured and they showed it over and over on replay.

So, find her connection. And never belittle other sports because they aren't ones you watch. Don't start saying how stupid golf or soccer is because you might just find out she does it every weekend. Even if you have rival teams, don't belittle her for cheering for them. A bit of good-natured teasing is fine, but make sure to keep it in check.

Last Resort

If you don't think anything will work and you don't know what to do...

Just ask her!

Just come right out and ask, no matter what the conversation has been like. It's a really simple thing to do and you don't have to lead up to it. If you felt like there was a connection, then just ask her.

Sometimes you just need to take a chance.

Chapter 10: How to Tell a Story, Joke, or Just Have a Conversation

Years ago, I did a few open mic nights at a local comedy club because I wanted to get over any fears I had of speaking in front of crowds. I worked up a few minutes and got a few laughs. It definitely wasn't for me, but it was a great experience.

I got to see a lot of comedians those nights and learned a lot from just watching. Not everybody is a great joke teller. Some people are just natural storytellers. But if that's not you, I have you covered.

To start, always know your audience. If you just walked up to her and she has a cross around her neck, you might not tell her a joke about a naughty priest. Always tell jokes that are appropriate to who is around. If you're going to tell a dirty joke at a wedding, make sure the six-year-old flower girl isn't standing nearby listening.

Keep it short and witty. Make sure it's pertinent to the situation. It comes off really weird to tell a joke about cows after they just told you the story of a car accident as a child.

Get it right. You don't want to screw up a punch-line or reveal.

Try starting off the joke as if it's something that really happened to you, then the punchline hits.

For example:

"I was in the hospital for six months, then they kicked me out because I thought it was a hotel."

Don't guffaw at your own joke, just offer a wry smile that you know it's funny.

Types of Humor

Everybody's sense of humor is a little different, including women. Some women like dry and witty, others like stupid jokes. Most are fans of a little off-color and innuendo humor. So, if you can figure out what type of a sense of humor they have really quickly, you're going to be far more successful at making her laugh.

It's also important that you know when you are bringing it up. If you go on and on about how funny The Three Stooges are and she hates them, that is going be in a strike against your instant connection.

Dry & Witty

The majority of women loves dry humor. Being able to deliver a line without a smile is a big thing. Women definitely find it sexy. It's about the control you have and the bit of aloofness when the line is delivered.

Being able to deliver a dry joke about someone while they are standing there and they don't know it is the ultimate prize for dry humor. It's almost guaranteed if a woman hears it, they will come up to you and want to mention it.

Poking Fun at Life

This is when you look for the absurd in the world. Laughing at small little things that pop up in life.

It's usually pretty light-hearted and a bit of a positive approach to life. Sort of the optimistic reverse of sarcasm.

Dark of Gallows Humor

Dark humor can be a bit... dark. Usually, it's jokes about death, dismemberment, or just not the natural way society looks at things. It can be fun, and to throw out a dark joke and maybe even comment afterward "Eh, a little too dark?" can be fun.

Slapstick

Broad humor often with physical. Women might like this but usually not from their men.

I knew a guy once who was really good at pratfalls. He could walk into walls, fall, and make it look like he hurt himself. He used to try to do it to impress girls. He would do it once and the girl shrieked, saw he was ok, and laughed. But then he would do it a bunch of times and by the end, she was annoyed. A group of us finally sat him down and told him we thought it was cool what he could do and girls did, too, but what made it cool was that he only got them once. After that, they didn't like it so much.

So, he changed it up and only did it once. He actually got this whole routine down. He would smack into a wall in front of a girl and while she thought he was hurt and others came over to see if he was ok, he would wink at her to let her know it was a joke. It created a bond and after he had "recovered", he would come over and talk to her about their secret. I have to give him credit, he turned himself around.

Self-Depreciating

This is not a type of humor you want to use very much when talking to women. You want to build yourself up and this can come across as a defense mechanism. You don't want to tear yourself down.

She might have this sense of humor as well but realize it might be her own defense measure. So, it isn't a good idea to pile on to her joke, and make sure that when you playfully tease her that might not be the topic to bring up.

Pop Culture References

We all do it to some degree, but some people do it like it was a second language. Don't do that when you're talking with a woman. Save that for hanging out with your buddies.

If you are going to use a reference or a line from a movie as a joke, make sure you do it in a cool way. Unless you have the world's greatest Arnold

Schwarzenegger impression, don't do a voice when you quote from his films. Try to just slip it into what you are saying with a little dramatic flair.

Part of the fun is seeing if she notices. If she catches it, it gives you a chance to tease her a bit about the fact she knew. If it's a superhero or comic book film, tease her about being a secret geek. If it's a comedy, tease her about being able to quote films. It's a great connector.

And don't do a theme of movie quotes the entire time you talk to her.

Sarcasm

This type of humor can be very dark and biting. An occasional sarcastic remark can be fun, but most people don't like to hang out with a sarcastic person too long.

Smart Jokes

These jokes require, well, smart content. They play on information about science, math, literature, and other areas of academia. It's a niche type of humor, so you should put in reserve for when you know that you're talking with a woman who will appreciate it. And never tell a smart joke you don't understand. Even if she doesn't understand it, she'll know if you don't.

Crude Humor

Proceed with caution here. Crude humor is exactly what it sounds like: crude. Some women will like it, others won't, and others will only like it (or tolerate it) depending on the setting and company. Don't assume that all women hate it. In fact, I know multiple women whose favorite jokes are crude.

Still, don't make this your go-to humor. If you use it without being absolutely certain that she likes it, you'll end up looking like a huge creep.

Identifying Her Sense of Humor

I started off this chapter by telling you to know your audience. This is key to making a woman laugh. To do that, though, you need to know what kind of humor she has. If you don't, you could potentially be faced with chirping crickets after delivering your punchline. And that's only if you don't inadvertently offend her.

Asking her directly, while it seems to be the easiest way, is also the most awkward. So, what should you do?

Humor isn't an exact science. There's no exact way to tell what someone will find funny until you get to know them better. Even after years of knowing each other, someone's sense of humor will surprise you. But there are a few things to focus on in a conversation to help you figure out the general sense of humor of a woman you're talking with.

What Has She Laughed At?

Obviously, what she has laughed at while you've been talking to her is a pretty good indicator of what she finds funny. Pay attention to what you say, what she says, and what those around you, if you are in a group, say that make her laugh. From there, you should be able to get a rough idea of her sense of humor.

Be careful, though. Many misunderstandings could sabotage this approach. Sometimes, people force a laugh in order to avoid an awkward situation. They might not want to hurt someone's feelings or fear feeling singled out because they don't "get it". Other times, people laugh out of nervousness or even due to a substance they're on (which would be a good thing to look out for also).

Still, you will probably be able to tell if the laughter is false, and if she seems to be laughing at the same kind of thing throughout the conversation, it's safe to say it's something she genuinely finds funny.

What Jokes Does She Tell?

Just like you'll be more likely to tell jokes that you think are funny, so will women. Pay attention to her jokes and they'll help reveal her type of humor.

But don't repeat her own jokes back to her. You can attempt what's called a "callback", which I'll tell you more about when we talk about how to tell a good story. Still, you'll want to only use her jokes as a guideline to her humor, not a strict rulebook.

What Shows and Movies Does She Like?

Does she like sitcoms and rom-coms? Adult cartoons? Late night sketch shows? What she likes to watch on both the small screen and the big screen can reveal a lot more about a woman than just her tastes in TV and film. For example, if she likes *The Three Stooges*, she probably prefers slapstick. Is *Bridesmaids* her favorite movie? Her guilty pleasure might be crude humor.

Even her preferences outside the comedy genre can help you piece together her comedic tastes. If she likes horror films, she might go for some dark of gallows humor. A woman who likes watching MTV will appreciate pop culture references.

As it usually is when trying to get to know someone, the trick to figuring out a woman's humor is to look at everything you learn about her together. Only then will you get close to the truth without directly asking her.

Practiced Variety

Even if you think you've figured out her sense of humor, don't play any single joke or type of humor to death. Remember my friend with the pratfall routine? He overused slapstick humor to his repeated failure. However, he was able to turn it around and come up with a one-and-done act that made him pretty popular with women.

You will want to stick with the sense of humor that most aligns with your own. That way, your jokes will come out more naturally and you will make connections with women who have senses of humor similar to yours. Yet you will also want to have a routine like my friend's ready for each type of humor, both as an icebreaker and for help in continuing a conversation. This will allow you to adjust your approach depending on the woman and be varied enough to keep her laughing, not rolling her eyes.

You'll want to practice your routine(s) before incorporating them into your conversations with women. Don't sound as rehearsed as a stand-up comedian, but make sure that you're familiar enough with your own jokes and routines to execute them smoothly, confidently, and at the appropriate times. Try them out on female friends and family members, and they'll let you know if the routines and jokes will work or if you just look like a clown.

And remember, a little spontaneity can be a good thing—just make sure that you're confident in your improv before you start, or else you'll end up with egg on your face.

How to Tell a Good Story

Personalize It

Find moments to make a connection with her by finding items that she has experienced. If you are telling her a story about high school, connect with her by saying something like "You remember what that was like..." to connect about something you both would have obviously experienced like lockers, gym class, or the cafeteria.

Figure Out Your Best Couple of Stories and Practice Them

We know the best stories that we have told our friends. They laughed or gasped and we knew as we told it they were in the palm of our hand.

Practice telling these stories. It's ok to tell it on every date or every time you are talking to a girl. Each time, play with the way you tell it. Don't change the story, but work on inflections and dramatic pauses. It will help you become a master storyteller.

Keep That Eye Contact

You are the star of a one-man show and she's your excited audience. Keep that eye contact as you tell your story.

Inject Some Emotion

Find the places where you can elicit emotion by creating a vivid picture. By adding a description, she will become more emotionally involved.

She's painting a picture in her mind and you are providing the paint. Say "I remember..." and tell her details. That will also trigger feelings in her that you are observant and will remember things about her.

Make Sure You Know Your Story

Just like telling a joke, storytelling is in the delivery. You could be perfect the entire way through and then flub the twist, or maybe you veer off on side stories or a dozen other ways to ruin a tale. Keep on narrative and know your story.

The Callback

A callback isn't what you think. It has nothing to do with her phone numbers or giving her a ring. It's about when you are talking and you "call back" to something you already talked about.

Let's say early in the conversation she told you that she tends to be a bit clumsy. In fact, sometimes she calls herself "Clumsy Carla" because of it. After you guys talk a little bit, she mentions that she recently hurt herself in a really silly way because she wasn't paying attention. So, you say something like "Well, it makes sense...I mean you are Clumsy Carla."

This is a great move. You did several things. First of all, you said something funny and she's going to laugh. By humorously teasing her, you made a fun connection.

You also did something else. You used your memory and made another personal connection amplifying the experience. By using the information and name she provided, you proved to her that not only do you listen, you process and understand what she says.

You can use this technique in many ways, but be careful not to drive it into the ground. Like with jokes, callbacks can get old. If you keep using the same one, she's going to start getting annoyed and bored with you.

How to Swear

When I was younger, one year I had a job working in the fields picking crops for summer. It was one of the hardest jobs I ever had, and I learned a lot about hard work, determination, and absolutely hating your boss.

My boss was a complete jerk. He was full of himself, arrogant, and loved to try to give us inspirational speeches before we were sent out into the fields with a bucket to fill. It was the most annoying part of the day.

However, I learned one thing from him that I still believe today. He didn't want to have his workers swearing. He didn't like it (he was a religious man) and he wouldn't stand for it. When you swear, he told us, you are just showing people how small your vocabulary is and how ignorant you really are.

Now, I admit I definitely swear. I like to let out a good curse word now and then. I also enjoy using a swear word as an adjective from time to time or as an exclamation. It's a punctuator.

It's also in the delivery. When you curse or use an F-bomb creatively and under control, you'll get the desired effect. By using it sparingly, it'll create a bit of stir when you do and will actually make her think you are a wise wordsmith.

Don't pepper your conversation with swearing, though. My old boss was right, you'll come across as having a small vocabulary and women will think you don't know how to express yourself with cursing. There are also some who just plain don't like it.

What if I Accidentally Swear?

Some people, men and women alike, have a hard time not swearing under certain circumstances. You might stub your toe, drop a glass, hit your head, pretty much any number of minor physical accidents and let out a curse. If you do, don't panic. It's not the end of your conversation, even if you're talking with a woman who disapproves of swearing.

First of all, apologize. I can't emphasize that enough. Even if she hasn't shown any signs of having a problem with cursing so far, this should be your automatic reaction whenever you let a bad word slip in public. It's just good manners. But don't say "I'm sorry". As I said earlier, "sorry" is overused in today's society to the point of losing all meaning. Instead, say something like "my bad" or "pardon me, I shouldn't have said that." More than anything, she'll appreciate your willingness to admit you were wrong. She might even tell you it was no big deal.

Then, play it off lightheartedly. Laugh and say something like, "Someone better get me some soap to wash out my potty mouth" or "No one tells my mom I have such a sailor mouth". If you're at a bar or somewhere else that serves alcohol, you might even consider the classic deadpan delivery of "I guess I've had one too many." If handled properly, it could lead to some more laughs and an opportunity for you to make jokes and callbacks later on. She might even join in and serve you some good-natured teasing.

Chapter 11: What You Can Learn from Sources Other Than Her

This is where you get to play a bit of the Sherlock Holmes game.

Sure, you've been listening to her and finding things out, but there are other ways to learn.

Her Appearance

Women take a great deal of pride in their appearance and their own personal style. So, first of all, a reminder to compliment them on the style, not just the appearance.

Her Purse

Is it high fashion? Is it more of a backpack? Does it have a big designer label or trademark? The type of purse she has says a lot about her. High style usually means high maintenance and possibly a preoccupation with money and trend. A backpack purse usually means a casual girl who is more into the guy.

Her Clothes and Shoes

It depends on where you are, but the fashion she is wearing will tell you a lot. Is she dressed to impress or is more about her own style and comfort? If she's wearing tighter clothing, it's usually a sign of high self-esteem and low body issues, which means she's fun and knows what she wants. Probably fewer games.

Often a woman (like a man) who wears baggy clothes has body issues. It doesn't mean they aren't great women, just be careful around certain subjects when you are talking until you get to know her a bit better.

Check her shoes, do they look stylish? If so, she could be a fashionista.

Of course, these are just guides. There are a lot of women who may be overcompensating, and they might wear tight clothes despite the low self-esteem. Similarly, many women wear baggy clothes because they care more about comfort than appearance rather than from any body issues.

Her Nails

Does she have a manicure? Are they long? Are they crazy colors? Comment and ask about them. If they are really crazy and colorful, it usually means they have a creative side. Ask her if she's artistic, you might have just found the perfect opening!

Her Jewelry

Is it simple? Or ornate? Simple and classy like pearls can tell you that she's got a refined sense of style, so cater your approach accordingly. Is she more arts and crafts with her jewelry? She's probably a bit more creative with a broader sense of humor.

Make sure to compliment her on her jewelry. Make sure it's unique and deserves the compliment, though.

How She Talks

You can learn a lot about someone by what they talk about, but have you considered *how* they say it? Listening to how someone talks is a very help-ful way to learn about them beyond what they say. It's the same for the woman you're talking with.

Does she speak formally or casually? Loudly or quietly? Is her vocabulary complex or simple? Does she swear, and if so, how much? All of these can speak volumes for her personality, upbring-ing, education level, and so on. You could even get a hint as to where she's from based on her accent. (But don't rely too heavily on these assumptions—it's very easy to mix up similar accents. Trust me, you don't want to ask a woman what part of Eng-land she's from and have it turn out that she's Australian.)

It's not just her voice and vocabulary that you should pay attention to. Watch her body language, too. More importantly, watch her *hands*. People will talk with their hands for a lot of reasons: they're nervous, they're excited, they're passionate about the subject, they're passionate about the person whom they're speaking to, etc. So, take subtle looks to see how much she talks with her hands. Any changes as the conversation goes on can help you learn more about her and adjust your strategy.

I remember that soon after graduating, I moved into a new apartment building. One of my neighbors was this gorgeous woman in her late twenties. For the first couple months, our conversations never got beyond a friendly greeting and maybe some chit-chat about the weather. One day during one of these doomed weather discussions, I let slip about how I hoped that everyone had brought their pets inside because of the heat advisory. Suddenly, an interesting transformation occurred in my neighbor: her hands, which had been pretty still up to this point, started to move rapidly as she started talking about how she hates when people don't keep their animals safe. It dawns on me that animals must be important to her if she was getting so animated about it, so I decided to steer the conversation in that direction.

That turned into the longest, most meaningful conversation we'd had up to that point. I learned about our mutual love of animals, how she had grown up on a farm, and that she was a vet tech at a nearby veterinary clinic. We both had to go to work but were so engaged in the conversation that we exchanged numbers. Nothing romantic came of it, but to this day, long after we moved to different cities, she's still one of my closest friends.

If you notice that she's moving her hands more when talking about a specific subject, take note.

Like with my former neighbor, it probably means that she has a particular passion for that topic, and following that subject will give you a more meaningful and productive conversation. You might even find a common interest more quickly than by just listening to her words.

Where You Met Her

Take notice of the location where you saw and met the woman. Is it a club or a bar? Or is it an event? You don't want to ask her if she comes here often, but try to find out if it's a regular thing she does.

If she seems knowledgeable about the location or event, odds are it's an interest of hers. Look around if this seems to be the case and see if there are things you can discuss. Even better, if she knows about the location, ask her questions so she can explain things to you. It will show her you respect her for her brain, not just her body, and help deepen the interaction.

Online

You can always check them out on Facebook, Instagram, and other platforms. People jokingly refer to it as "Internet stalking," but everybody does it and it's a great tool to use. Just keep in mind that there is a very fine line between "checking someone out" and genuinely stalking them. If it feels wrong or like an invasion of their privacy, stop. It's your gut raising a red flag, and you better not ignore it.

Also, be careful on LinkedIn because it can show the person who has been checking them out.

Her Friends

Use this sparingly, carefully, and, honestly, quite skillfully. You don't want to come right out and ask questions. Try to be a bit sly in your questioning of her friends, especially if you aren't very well acquainted with them.

If they come right out and say something to you about how she has noticed you or is interested, be cool about it. Let them know you are interested but don't show too much interest. Just enough to let them know you are genuine.

Your Female Friends

If you don't have friends who are female, you really should. I don't care what the movies say, men and women can just be friends.

It might be a co-worker, a male friend's longtime girlfriend or just someone you know. Nobody knows women better than other women.

They aren't going to know everything about how each particular woman thinks, but your female friends can give you a lot of insight as to why a woman might have reacted to a specific thing you did or didn't do or how she might react differently.

Take my former neighbor. One night, we went out to this bar popular with people in their twenties and thirties. There was this really cute girl at the bar, so I sat next to her and started chatting her up while my neighbor sat a couple stools away talking with some friends from work. I thought things were going well, but after a while, I could feel the conversation starting to stall. I kept trying to revive it but gave up after a few minutes and went back to my neighbor. I started griping about how I don't get why I have a hard time hitting it off with women when I'm such a nice guy. (First mistake: never go down the "nice guy" road with women. To see why, check out my book, *How to Attract Women*.)

My neighbor decided to cut me off and give it to me straight. She pointed out to me that there were actually a lot of red flags that the woman I had been talking to was uncomfortable with me. Whenever I leaned towards her, she would lean away from me. When I would reach across her to grab some peanuts from the bowl set on the counter, the woman would cringe and shrink away. If I ever talked above normal conversation volume, she would pull into herself. My neighbor explained that even though she didn't know for sure what the other woman had been through, it was clear that she had problems with personal space and loud noises. To my neighbor, that signaled that the woman might have been abused or had similar issues in her personal relationships.

If it hadn't been for my neighbor, I never would've noticed those subtle hints. Because she was a woman, she could spot obvious signs of discomfort in the other woman and even come to a reasonable explanation for why she might be that way. Now, not only do I pay more attention to women's body language, but the first people I turn to for advice when an interaction with a woman has gone south are my female friends.

Female friends are great to bounce questions off and get the woman's view on things. Talk to them. Use their knowledge.

A Word of Caution

Remember, all of these are just pieces of the puzzle. Don't make too many assumptions based on one or two of these aspects alone. Like Sherlock

Holmes who takes into account every detail and changes his conclusions with each new clue, look at everything that you learn about a woman all together. If you find something that seems to contradict your previous beliefs, adjust your view of her accordingly. There's always more than meets the eye.

Chapter 12: Online and Texting Conversations

So much of our life takes place through texts, apps, and online. We pay our bills, shop, and find love.

The rules of having online conversations are a bit different than person-to-person. Sometimes you can push subjects into a sexier territory, while other times you have to be careful that what you wrote isn't taken out of context.

If you can learn how to maneuver through the digital world, you have the opportunity to have amazing conversations full of flirting and fun that will lead to dates and more.

Texting

Texting is a huge part of how we communicate, but too easily, misunderstandings can arise. Many of these can be avoided by following a few dos and don'ts.

Texting Dos

- Always double-check what you write before sending. It's just nice to check grammar and send something readable, but you also don't want to accidentally send her a message whose meaning was changed because you used the word "sex" instead of "six".

- If you haven't texted them before, make sure you mention who it is in the first message.

- Mention your texting habits casually. Let her know if you are always on your phone or tend to leave it aside while you are doing things. That way, she'll know how you tend to text. Try to learn her style as well.

- Save the big conversations for in person. Plant some seeds with some flirting and comments, but if you have big questions or want to delve into a subject, wait until you are face to face.

- It's ok to send a funny photo or selfie, but don't hit them with a dozen all at once. Also, make sure you are clothed in any selfie you send.

- Move the conversation forward. Don't dwell on topics or keep going back to the same line or joke.

- Do use innuendo! But make sure it is clever and never crude.

Texting Don'ts

- Don't bombard her with texts without waiting for a response.

- Don't spread your message out over numerous texts. Be concise.

- Don't include the person in mass texts. It's annoying to most people, let alone someone you are trying to get to know. Everyone in the mass text is going to see what the reader sends. Flirting, and anything to do with sex, can be seen by many, and this can cause a lot of embarrassment.

- Don't go crazy with the emojis. Also, make sure you know what the slang means before you use it.

- Don't drag a text conversation out if you aren't understanding each other. Sometimes you just need to call someone to make things clear.

- Don't play the waiting game. If you got a text from her, answer her back when you know what to say and have a safe opportunity (as in don't text and drive).

- Don't get sarcastic or too dry with your humor. This can be easily lost in texts and should be saved for in-person meetings.

- Don't text her in the middle of the night. Some people don't turn their phones off because they need to be accessible. Texting her in the middle of the night could get you into some hot water.

Be careful texting a woman whose number you got through a mutual friend. Women often consider this a rather cowardly move as they wonder why you didn't have the guts to come up to them and talk to them in person. It might even be construed as creepy and stalkerish. Instead, approach the woman in person first and get her number directly from her. She'll appreciate that you aren't playing games with her and will feel much safer talking with you in text.

Dating Apps and Sites

Traditional Dating Sites (Match, OK Cupid, etc.)

There are a lot of different apps and websites out there now. Some are all about the quick hook up, while others are a bit deeper and are meant to help you find "The One."

The way you talk to them is going to be a bit different as well. It's not just about the app or the goal but also the woman you are talking to.

Flirting is going to go to be very important here. You can usually push things a little bit more with the innuendo after a few back-and-forths, but you want to be sly and witty. Don't just come right out and say things, hint at it.

Make sure you stay in the conversation and move it forward organically. Don't jump subjects or get too many conversation threads going at once. If that does happen and you have so much you are talking about, it's a great reason to set up a time to go out together.

Don't drag it out too long. If you haven't set a date after a few days of chatting, your odds are going to go down. Remember she's still getting messages from other guys while you two talk. If you don't move things along, another guy will!

Dating Apps (Tinder, Bumble, etc.)

Swiping

There are a lot of approaches to swiping on these apps. One of them is to just swipe on every girl to get all the matches that you can. In order to do this, you have to pay for a membership package or you will be limited to a certain number of swipes per day. This way, you'll get more matches and have higher odds.

The other is to go slower and actually read the profiles and swipe based on the actual physical and mental attraction to the women. Your odds are lower of matches, but the ones that you get are going to be real matches based on your attraction and interest.

I see why people would want to go swipe happy and I don't blame them, but I have one reason I don't think you should.

I think women are really amazing. All women. I don't want to sleep with everyone, but I love and appreciate everything about them. I think that's part of the reason I have been able to learn so much about interacting with them. I think that when you swipe blindly, you aren't getting to know the women and giving them the respect they deserve.

You can become "attraction desensitized" and lose part of the thrill of the hunt. If you actually swipe on them purposefully and then get a match, it's a deeper meaning and more fun. You have more invested and you are going to go after her with more confidence and passion. And we've talked about how women react to those.

Not to mention, you just created a lie and you haven't even met them yet. They are going to ask you... MARK MY WORDS... what was it about their profile that attracted you to them. So, either you tell them you were swiping blindly or you lie to her. Not a great thing to do.

- Get your messages out quickly. Don't wait or take your time. Speed is of the essence. Women tend to get a lot of matches on Tinder, and if you wait, a bunch of other guys are going to get to her first.

- Don't use a cutesy "false nervous" approach in your first message. Here's an example of this approach:

Hi, it's um *looks down at feet* nice to, um, meet you. You know, you're, uh, really, you know, pretty *laughs nervously*. I saw that we matched on here and thought, well, that maybe you'd like to talk. *sweats profusely*

Men—and women, although that's rare—who use this think that it's "adorable" or "endearing". Maybe they think it'll make them seem non-threatening when, in fact, it contains a lot of red flags, starting with its lack of confidence. This trend seems to be rising both in text and in dating apps lately, and it's not really cute. It's annoying, a bit creepy, and a waste of time.

- Make sure you read her entire profile! She might have kids, be looking for something specific, or not even be a woman! There are a lot of transgender people on apps and you might not know it. Look for clues like the term "TS", "TG" or offhand comments like "The University of Manila (or other Philippines or Thailand locations).

- Get to the date, don't wait forever. If you haven't asked her out within a few days, odds are, she's going to move on. They aren't looking to make online pen pals; they are looking to meet men like you.

- Compliment her on things other than her looks. Tinder and other similar sites are based on appearances, it's just the way it's set up. You swipe based on what you see and a few lines of a profile. So, most comments that women get are going to be very superficial. Stand out by commenting on other things in the photo or her profile. Look for interesting ways to comment on her pet, the location, or what she is doing in the image.

- Keep it fun and flirty. Much like texting, don't ask massive long questions. Save that for your face-to-face meeting.

- Don't make sex jokes right away. Test the water a bit and it might even wait until you meet in person. However, if she says something sexual (and women can be very forward on apps), don't shy away, give her innuendo right back.

- Never start a conversation by just saying "Hello" or "Hi." Say something interesting. Say something funny. Make her want to write back to you.

- Don't send her a bunch of messages before she has a chance to write back. Send her one nice introduction (with some fun or flirty undertones) and wait for her to respond.

- Don't create a false reality. Her picture may be gorgeous. She may sound like you have all the same interests and you'll be perfect for each other. But don't build her up too much based upon a small amount of information.

- We know people might lie on these profiles. It's ok to exaggerate a bit, but out and out, lies happen. If they didn't, catfishing wouldn't be a thing. So, don't get caught in a lie, either.

- Don't call someone you have never met by a name you think is cute. No babe, baby, cutie, beautiful, darling, and the like.

- Even if everything she wrote was accurate, it's only part of what and who she is. She could love the same sports team you do as well as the same food and be gorgeous, but once she opens her mouth in person, you could be turned off by every word that comes out of her mouth.

- Offer information but don't dominate. You want to have a conversation that leads her to be interested and want to know more, but you can't just kick back and expect her to ask all the right questions. Offer hints and breadcrumbs of interesting information so she'll come to you for more.

- So, enjoy the fun of the conversation, but don't get invested until you meet up.

If It Doesn't Go Well, Don't Be a Jerk

Once, I was chatting with a really nice woman on one of the apps and I thought things were moving ahead great. We had set a time to meet for coffee and I thought we were going to have a great time.

Suddenly, I got a message and she said that she had rethought it all and while I seemed like a great guy, she was going to have to turn down the date and end the conversation. She wished me luck and that was the last I heard from her.

Now, she has every right to back out. I have absolutely no idea what her reasoning was. She might have made another date, decided she wasn't that into me, maybe she didn't like my hair. I have no idea, but it doesn't matter.

You can't get hung up if a woman slips away. You have to roll with it and move on. Never get angry or feel hurt and especially never take it out on them. Don't send threatening messages or say that they don't know what they are missing. Act like an adult. You can send them a nice message saying "I totally get it. No harm. Best wishes in your search!" And that's it. Let it lie.

You can't take it personally, especially online. We never know what's really going on with people behind keyboards. Just keep moving forward. Always remember that anything can become viral. If you say something negative in response, this could become a viral thread on social media, marking your profile as a jerk forever.

Honestly, it might just be the wrong time. You might meet them again and find out it was nothing about you and you can pick up right where you left off!

I remember a time when the brother of one of my female friends went through a really nasty breakup after his girlfriend cheated on him. They had been together for five years, lived together, the whole nine yards, and it did not end cleanly. This left him depressed and bitter at women in general for a long time. Rather than waiting for himself to cool down and take time to grieve the breakup, he let some of his buddies convince him to join Tinder and try to rebound (rarely a good idea). He hit it off with this one woman and arranged to meet her at a nearby coffee shop. He was stoked.

The night before the date, he got a message from the woman telling him that she's sorry but that she had "done some soul-searching" and didn't feel that "now's the right time for her to date again". No big deal, right? Well, he didn't take it so calmly and immediately sent her a series of messages accusing women of "all being alike" and of her being a lot of bad words and comparing her to his ex. Then he blocked her. He immediately regretted his rage, but it was too late. Snapshots of the conversation were sent around the internet, and even my friend gave her brother an earful for what he did.

The kicker is that in the thread, the woman mentioned how she had really been having a great time with him. For her, it was just about timing. She had just started a new job in a new city and had been in a funk, severely homesick. She didn't want to get too serious with a guy until she was settled in comfortably and certain she wouldn't change her mind and go back to her hometown.

If my friend's brother had just given himself time to calm down before responding and ignored his knee-jerk reaction to it, he wouldn't have been blackballed among women so severely. He might have even had a second chance with her or could have become good friends with her if he had just responded with understanding—or, at least, not like a jerk.

While this is a more extreme reaction, it's not far from par for the course when it comes to the negative reactions women's rejections face online. You never know what's going on in someone's life, so don't take online rejections so personally and especially do not take out your own problems on the woman who rejected you.

Chapter 13: How to Talk to Women in Other Countries

Traveling is no reason to suddenly stop talking to women! In fact, meeting and talking with women in other countries can be an amazing experience.

Even aside from potential romance, it's a way to learn about the world, other cultures, and practice your conversational skills.

Living Overseas

As I've said before, I've had the pleasure of traveling around the world. I've also lived while I've worked in certain countries for a few months at a time. If you get the opportunity, I would highly recommend it.

If you are just looking to live overseas for a few months or maybe a year, becoming an ESL teacher is a great option. In some countries, it pays really well and you are provided with travel and accommodations, and you still have a lot of time to socialize with the locals.

If you are looking for something more adventurous, cargo ships and container vessels often look for crews in exchange for a salary, room, and board. You can cross the ocean in about two and a half weeks and have enough to have some fun or go on to the next port.

How to Approach Women Abroad

This is going to be different from country to country. In *How to Flirt with Women,* I discussed some of the differences in cultures and body languages in other countries. Every place is going to be different.

The easiest way is simply walking up with a smile and saying hello. As long as you are polite and unassuming, you are most likely going to have a pleasant experience.

Note, make sure you understand how things work in the country you visit. There are some where it is considered improper for women to be approached by or for them to talk to strange men.

Hostels

Depending on where you are staying and what your budget and lifestyle are, you might want to consider hostels. They are an especially prudent option in Southeast Asian countries like Thailand, where "begpacking"—a technique often used by Western tourists without enough money to fund their trips—is discouraged and often illegal. You'll meet people from around the world right where you are staying, and many of them will be able to help you make social connections in the city or be looking to make friends and go out.

There are often lots of bars and clubs near hostels where you can meet your fellow travelers and the locals. However, the living quarters at the hostel might not be ideal if the opportunity comes to bring a girl home with you.

Language Barrier

One thing that you have going for you is that English is one of the most widely spoken languages on the planet. So, this means the odds are that any woman you want to talk to will know at least a few words of English.

In most countries, English is very prevalent, especially with younger people. In many Asian and European countries, they speak multiple languages, including English. They also often want to practice with a native-born English speaker, so that means they want to talk to you!

Speak slowly and clearly so she can understand you but at a speed that is comfortable and confident. Slang doesn't always translate, even when they speak English. By using too much of it, you are risking alienating her or her becoming frustrated. Also, remember, slang can mean different things in different countries.

Dialogue and phrase books are great as well as apps for your smartphone that help translate. Also, make sure to double check any translations that you do online because these are not always accurate and can lead to some embarrassing mistranslations. I always like to make sure I am carrying a pen so I can draw something that I am talking about. Another trick is to have a drawing app on your phone so you can sketch out a quick picture.

Don't Shout

We all have a horrible tendency to do this. If we aren't being understood, instead of repeating ourselves slowly and maybe changing some tough words, we just say it again louder.

This is rude and is a great way to end the conversation very quickly! You might even scare a woman off by doing that. Slow down and repeat yourself, but not so much it seems you are mocking them. Just realize they are doing the best they can. **Offer to have them teach you some language and laugh if you don't get it!**

Make Sure She Understands

Don't be rude, but ask nicely if she understood what you said. She might not want to admit that she didn't and is just letting you talk. Keep your sentences short so she can ask questions or for you to repeat yourself.

Also, be careful of saying "Did you hear me" or any variation where you say "hear." In many Asian countries, they are very literal. They will say yes because they heard the sound of what you said, but it doesn't mean they understood you.

Use Body Language

As you are talking, point to things or make motions that punctuate and back up what you said. Be careful, though, because in some countries, large gestures are considered very rude.

Check out my book *How to Flirt with Women* for more information on how to break the ice and what gestures or body language to avoid in foreign countries. Also, in *How to Attract Women*, I talk about what women abroad find especially unique and sexy about foreign men.

Online

I'm definitely not telling you to meet someone online and then travel there or you might end up with a pretty disappointing surprise. However, once you are there, you can use apps like Tinder to meet local women.

Once they see you are from another country, the chances are they will be very intrigued and swipe right on you. Be prepared to explain why you are visiting, and looking for sex is not an answer!

Watch the Local Men

Go to a coffee shop or café and watch how men interact with women in the area. You'll get an idea of what is expected, what is liked and what isn't.

Ask Her to Be Your Guide

A great way to get to know a woman in a foreign country is to ask if she can show you around. It's a great way to get a personal look at a foreign city, but you will also be able to spend quality time together and have some great conversations. Who knows where it might lead?

It's her country and culture and it means a lot to her. When she shares things with you, it helps to create a personal connection, which can move things forward quickly.

Don't Assume

There are stereotypes about women from different countries on whether they will have sex with you quickly or not. In my experience, it's partially true.

I find European women have been more sexually liberated than other regions, and Australian women have been very good to me. But I have definitely met some wonderful women from Russia, Asia, South America, and the rest of the world.

The truth is that if you understand and respect their culture and make a personal connection, just like with all women, **anything is possible.**

Travel Carefully

In addition to being careful not to offend women and avoid getting either of you in trouble, you must be on alert for your own safety. If you aren't on alert when talking to women in a new country, embarrassing yourself could be the least of your worries.

I had a friend who travelled to Greece on business one summer. He had some free time before his meeting, so he went to the local market and started talking up a cute girl. By the time he was done and on his way to the meeting, his wallet was missing from his back pocket along with his IDs and over USD$200 in local currency. The market had been pretty crowded, so he didn't know who had taken it or if the woman he had been talking to had at all been involved. After much to-do with the local police, he got his wallet and IDs back but not the money.

My friend was lucky to have gotten most of his stuff back. It can be difficult, to say the least, to get help when you're in a country you've never been to before, especially if you don't speak the language. And thievery isn't even the worst thing that can happen to you.

I'm not saying to never travel or never speak to the locals. In fact, you'll be doing yourself a disservice if you do this. Travel when you can, speak to whoever catches your interest, and experience things and meet people you could have never imagined otherwise. Not only could you meet wonderful women abroad, but your stories abroad can also help you connect with women at home.

However, keep your guard up. Even when you're talking to a beautiful woman, be aware of your surroundings. Don't look constantly over your shoulder or appear suspicious; that will weird the woman out at best, more likely scare her away. Just don't become so relaxed that you're an easy mark.

One Last Reminder Before Conclusion

Have you grabbed your free resource?

A lot of information has been covered in this book. As previously shared, I've created a simple mind map that you can use *right away* to easily understand, quickly recall and readily use what you've learned in this book.

If you've not grabbed it...

Click Here To Get Your Free Resource

Alternatively, here's the link:

https://viebooks.club/freeresourcemind-mapforhowtotalktowomen

Your Free Resource Is Waiting..

Get Your Free Resource Now!

Conclusion

So, you should now feel completely confident having a conversation with any woman. Everything I have laid out in this book has worked for me, and it will for you, as long as you listen and be confident and genuine.

The more engaged you are in conversation, the more you will benefit. The skills that you have learned in this guidebook will help you to see the best results with talking to women. You can employ many of them at your work and in your business circles.

It gives me great pleasure to share my knowledge with you. I had to make a lot of mistakes in my life talking with women, and I hope that by reading these books, you can learn without having to go through what I have.

The bottom line is this: If you have confidence in yourself and are a genuine person with a positive mindset and an interesting life, you will have no problem with women. Just be the best self you can be, whether it's a Lone Wolf, an adventurer, or a leader.

I would like to suggest you check out my two other books, *How to Flirt with Women* and

How to Attract Women. They have insight on how to break the ice and flirt as well as how to present yourself and make yourself as attractive as possible to women.

Best of luck, guys!

Sincerely,

Ray Asher

P.S.

If you've found this book helpful in any way, a review on Amazon is greatly appreciated.

This means a lot to me, and I'll be extremely grateful.

More Books By Ray Asher

How to Flirt with Women: The Art of Flirting Without Being Creepy That Turns Her On! How to Approach, Talk to & Attract Women (Dating Advice for Men)

How To Flirt With Any Woman Successfully – <u>The Ultimate Guide</u>

Are you unhappy with your dating life?

Are you craving female attention and sex, but not getting them?

Do you secretly feel unattractive because of some rejections you've faced in the past?

If you want to stop all these in your life, then keep reading...

Research shows that most women – even those who appear tough – are secretly looking for romance.

But no matter how you look like, how much money you have, or how muscular your body is...if you don't know **how to <u>flirt</u> with women**, you'll appear as:

- Needy

- Desperate

- Boring

- Lacking social intelligence

- Simply ...unattractive.

Flirting is the art of small talk. It includes a lot of playfulness, smooth conversation skills, and high social intelligence. In fact, with the right words, right tonality, and right "approach" – you can make ANY woman highly attracted to you.

In this book, **Ray Asher will show you how to flirt like a pro**.

Ray Asher used to be an introverted teenager who didn't have the courage to approach girls. He started dating a girl he liked in college – only to find she was cheating on him regularly. His pain drove him to go out every night and day, speak with women, and discover what makes them attracted. After thousands of rejections, a few "friends with benefits" and lots of notes – he discovered the power of flirting, and decided to share his knowledge with any men who wishes to become good with women.

This book is the most comprehensive guide ever written about flirting.

Here's a taste of what you'll discover inside *How to Flirt with Women*:

- Exactly what to say to make a conversation flirty and amusing

- Tonality tricks that make you look confident, funny and charismatic

- Four crucial principles of flirting that work for all women of all cultures

- How to create a "leader" frame in every conversation you have with women, and make them respect you

- The EXACT words and gestures that impress women

- How to text a girl and how to flirt online (with detailed tips for every social network)

- Techniques on how to approach and talk to women in different places and different social situations (at work, while traveling, at restaurants, farmers' markets – you name it!)

And much, much more...

Q: "But how can I be sure this book will work FOR ME?"

The dating advice for men in this book was written from experience, and was proven to work for people all over the world. Flirting is simply a way to transfer sexual emotions, it can work in any language with any woman. Readers who have tried the information in this book were SHOCKED to see how effective it is, even those virgins and those who never approached a woman before. If they can do it – SO CAN YOU!

Just buy the book, read the information and EX-ECUTE!

If you're ready to finally learn the art of flirting with women and become an attractive guy, now is the time.

How to Attract Women: Laugh Your Way to Effortless Dating & Relationship! Attracting Women By Knowing What They Want In A Man (Female Psychology for Understanding Them)

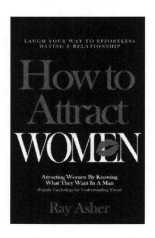

Do You Really, Really, REALLY Know What Women Want in a Man?

Are you single against your will?

Do you struggle when attracting women?

Do you feel that all the women you like are out of your league?

If you want to stop all these in your life, then keep reading...

Women don't care about that fancy pickup line you've found on the internet. They don't want to be put on a pedestal and blindly adored.

However, there are behaviors and skills that attract them like flowers attract bees – and they're often not the behaviors YOU think are sexy.

When Ray Asher started dating, he was unpopular with women. He tried being nice, being mean, playing games, wearing the latest fashions, memorizing sophisticated pickup lines... but nothing worked. Therefore, he began studying women to discover what they REALLY want in a man... and came to many surprising discoveries!

In *How to Attract Women*, you will discover the secrets to attract women from every city on the planet, create sharp sexual tension with the hottest women in the world, and build a relationship with the woman of your dreams!

Here's a taste of what you'll discover inside *How to Attract Women*:

- Women want a Good Guy, not a Nice Guy – learn the difference and show women how Good you are!

- Some of the behaviors you would call "masculine" actually scare women away – get to know and learn them!

- Women are attracted to certain skills and hobbies – learn exactly what skills are worth practicing and demonstrating

- Discover the one proven method to kill approach anxiety once and for all

- Train yourself to become confident – just read the step-by-step guide, put it into action and enjoy being confident around women!

- Understand how to text, talk and communicate in a seductive way

- Discover what women actually enjoy in bed and avoid mistakes that could ruin your relationship!

And much, much more...

Virgins became pickup artists...Heartbrokens to finding the love of their lives...friend-zoned to a player...this book will give you all the knowledge you need, all you have to do is EXECUTE.

Can you imagine your life with core confidence and abundance of women? If one man made it – then you can, too. Now it's your time.